LANDSCAPE OF GHOSTS

Bill Holm
Essays

Bob Firth
Photography

VOYAGEUR PRESS

Bill Holm

For my fellow semi-retired opera star, Diane, I never did get out of Minnesota as you see by this book. Enjoy Bill

Think Back...

Designed by John Weidman
Edited by Elizabeth Knight
Desktop Design by Patrick Wilson, TBW, Inc.

Printed in Hong Kong
93 94 95 96 97   5 4 3 2 1

Library of Congress Cataloging-in-Publication Data
Holm, Bill, 1943-
    Landscape of ghosts / text by Bill Holm ; photographs by Bob Firth
        p.   cm.
    ISBN 0-89658-198-5
    1. United States—Pictorial works. 2. United States—Social life and customs—20th century. 3. United States—Social life and customs—20th century—Pictorial works. 4. United States—Rural conditions. 5. United States—Rural conditions—Pictorial works. 6. Landscape—United States—Pictorial works. 7. Waste products—United States—Pictorial works.
    I. Firth, Bob. II. Title.
E169.04H65 1993
973.92—dc20   93-13595
                                                          CIP

Published by:
VOYAGEUR PRESS, INC.
P.O. Box 338, 123 North Second Street, Stillwater, MN 55082 U.S.A.

Please write or call, or stop by, for our free catalog. Our TOLL-FREE number to place an order or to obtain a free catalog is 800-888-9653 (or 612-430-2210 from Minnesota and Canada).

Educators, fundraisers, premium and gift buyers, publicists, and marketing managers: Looking for creative products and new sales ideas? Voyageur Press books are available at special discounts when purchased in quantities, and special editions can be created to your specifications. For details contact the marketing department.

We would like to thank the many poets whose work appears in *Landscape of Ghosts*.

Ruins and Eagle Feathers: A First Word with the Reader
"Love for Other Things," copyright 1993 by Tom Hennen
"Homesteader," from *Minnesota Gothic*, copyright 1992 by Mark Vinz. Published by Milkweed Editions, St. Paul, MN.
Poem by David Ignatow. Reprinted by permission of the author.

How to Take a Walk
"Der Vereinigten Staaten" by Johann Wolfgang von Goethe, translated by Robert Bly, from *Party Poems Touching on Recent American History*, copyright 1971 by Robert Bly. Published by Sixties Press.
"How to Take a Walk," from *Old Man Brunner Country*, copyright 1987 by Leo Dangel. Published by Spoon River Poetry Press, Granite Falls, MN.

Paint: A Moral Question
"Old Boards," from *Silence in the Snowy Fields*, copyright 1962 by Robert Bly. Published by Wesleyan University Press, Middleton, CT.

The Ghost under the Necessary House
"Outhouse Poem," from *Moon on the Fencepost*, copyright 1984 by Robert Bly. Published by Unicorn Press.
"Who Didn't Want an Indoor Toilet," from *Rescue the Dead*, copyright 1968 by Jim Heynen. Published by Wesleyan University Press, Middleton, CT.

The Virgin on the Farmall—The Venus in the Chevy
"Cottonwoods," from *Sacred Hearts*, copyright 1985 by Phebe Hanson. Published by Milkweed Editions, St. Paul, MN.

The Last Insult of the Glacier
"Picking Rock," from *The Man with Red Suspenders*, copyright 1986 by Phil Dacey. Published by Milkweed Editions, St. Paul, MN.

Petrified Chin Music
"Chin Music," by John Rezmerski. Reprinted by permission of the author.
"Poem Found Crossing Minnesota and South Dakota," by John Rezmerski. Reprinted by permission of the author.

Cutting Slices Out of the Wind
"Pictures of Three Seasons," from *Pictures of Three Seasons: A Collection of Poems*, copyright 1991 by Gail Rixen. Published by New Rivers Press, Minneapolis, MN.

Towers Rising from the Floor of the Sky
"The Silos," copyright 1990 by Nancy Paddock. First published in the *North Stone Review*
Poem from *The Man from Coal Lake*, copyright 1984 by David Bengston. Published by Scythe Press.

From Bill Holm,

To
Kathleen & Lawrence Owen and
Norma & Elmer Suderman,

my teachers
thirty years ago, and
my friends ever since,
who have fed me ideas, dinner, stories, music,
and the strong notion that both your work
and your life improve with love, humor,
paying attention to everyday life,
and practicing a firm spirit
of
contrariness.

———————

Bill Holm would like to thank:

Phyllis Yoshida, who typed these essays in Seattle while I wrote them in
Minneota. She is the fastest, wittiest computer in the West;

Virgil and Marnie Gislason, who lent me Hardware Hank's
fax machine at all hours of the night;

Gordon Brekken, for his sage advice on old cars;

Marc Wignes, for stories along with lunch at the M&M cafe;

Ron Yoshida, of Seattle Screenprint, for high-tech help;

Perry Lueders, who knows more about rock piles
than an opera lover should;

Carol Bly, for design consulting on outhouse carpentry,
and strong questions on content;

Elizabeth Knight, who did a brave job
trying to root out cant and bad diction; and

John Rezmerski, as always, for doing his best to
make me a little more intelligent with his editing pencil.

From Bob Firth,

To
my parents
for believing in me . . .

Bob Firth Sr.,
whose intellectual and artistic nature taught me the values of
knowledge, perseverance, creativity and perfection, and the rewards
of independence, self-reliance and self-motivation;

Alva Nash Duryea Firth,
for her patience in teaching me about love and compassion,
honesty, respect, and listening. Who always found something good
about almost anything or anyone, and gave me the freedom and
vision to see the beauty of other things.
I love you both.

———————

Bob Firth would like to thank:

Greg Snell, for turning on the light in a darkroom;

Patrick Wilson, computer genius and lifelong friend,
for art-full input and design, and for channeling powerful
computer spirits, and in memory of his father, Thomas B. Wilson;

John Weidman, friend, artist, book designer and
consultant extraordinaire. A voice from the wilderness of restraint,
good taste and excellence;

Bill Holm, an Icelandic American icon,
for the honor of his friendship;

Gary Gernbacher, Angie Raskob, Phil Mueller, and Ann Woodbeck.
Your knowledge, your help, your friendship;

My Children . . . Missi, Heidi, Tyler, Croix, and Buck,
who know that even when I'm there, I'm often someplace else;

And especially my wife, Nancy
who lets me go out to play.

Ruins and Eagle Feathers:
A First Word with the Reader

Here is a book full of pictures of stuff nobody wants to look at and of essays on subjects no one wants to read about. There's a sentence designed to help you save your money! Still, there may be something here, if you look or think twice.

Bob Firth called me a couple of years ago and asked if I wanted to do a picture book with him. After looking with delight at his pictures, I agreed. They are technically exact, imaginative, full of life, humor, love of light, and detail. Like any professional photographer who intends to make a living, Bob spends most of his professional life taking what I call postcard and calendar pictures: sunset on pristine lakes, snow in pine branches, loons fooling around in the boundary waters, melodramatic thunderheads roiling over a pastoral landscape. Tourists in airports, magazines, ad companies, gift shops, buy these pictures in staggering numbers. These pictures are often lovely; they are bread and butter; they are what citizens want to promote in their own landscape—the best face—but they do not include, as Paul Harvey says, the rest of the story.

Bob Firth didn't send me those pictures; he left them in Minneapolis. He sent me instead a box of transparencies that includes many of the pictures you see in this book: a ruined red farm truck by moonlight, a single white gravestone with two bare trees lit by some apocalyptic surrealist, a broken fallen-off windmill wheel, the trunk of an old green car sticking out of a weathered shed, faded Spearmint and radiator ads painted onto the bricks of old buildings, broken windows in a ruined masonry wall, an empty grain elevator lit up by dusk, a mammoth old barn with a fifteen percent lean, a rusted hayrake, a close-up shot of chipped bleached ancient paint on the wall of a deserted granary.

Now here was junk—and here was genius, too. Bob Firth is as much a prospector as he is a photographer, finding beauty where few others think to look. The affection and passion in these pictures was immediately clear to me and will become clear to you, too, if you give them a look. You can be sure that no mall promotion shots will ever come from this book. No tourist vacationing in canoe country will send a single one of these postcards home to Philadelphia. These pictures are for an audience of psychic heroes who are not afraid of decay, collapse, rust, grief, solitude and history. For you, maybe? We'll see. There's humor and tenderness too, as rewards if you can get past either your disapproval of ruins or your desire to make them into nostalgia for the good old days of iron wheels, horse farming, outdoor plumbing and picturesque red wood barns. Bob Firth is not Norman Rockwell; he has a jeweler's eye, not a peddler's.

I asked why he wanted me to write about this old junk. "Anyone who can crank out books about boxelder bugs and the Icelanders of Minneota must be an aficionado of useless old junk."

"I'm your man," I said. I hope I have done some justice to these fine pictures.

But this is not primarily a book of commentary on Bob Firth's photographs, though I have mentioned a few of them as metaphors. These pictures are their own description and stand up for themselves alone very nicely, thank you. I am a moralist, a harper on history and the necessity for humans to grow into a consciousness of it. I think no object is without the bricks of human history weighing it down, planting it on the earth as our neighbor. There is no weathered window without the ghost of a face behind it, no empty stanchion in a barn without a spectral cow munching hay and swishing her tail while a boy sits on a three-legged stool squeezing into a pail, no rusty iron tractor seat that doesn't remember the scratching of bib overalls against it.

Pure wilderness, if it exists at all, doesn't interest me. Until Kilroy (or Peterson or Jerzak) gets here, and leaves some record, a place is either stone dead or not yet come down the birth canal. I am an unapologetic human; my kind left these tracks. Some all right, some not, but tracks anyway . . . Sometimes I think I would rather shoot a wolf or a hawk than intrude on their private mating or hunting with a long hidden lens. They don't, after all, come into our bedrooms and kitchens to study our peculiar and private human habits, and speculate on preserving and managing us. It's all right to eat animals; they do us the same favor, and find us sometimes delicious, but we owe nature some courtesy, too, and ought to mind our own business more often than we do. These pictures show you the leavings of your own kind (*kin* in old English), and these essays ask you to think about the ghosts of those kin moving around them.

These are remnants, leavings, droppings. The title of this preface comes from Robert Schumann who used it in a review of Frederic Chopin's Preludes. The pieces are little chips, glimpses, fragments—sometimes only a few seconds long—"ruins and eagle feathers," Schumann called them. Most critics of the day wanted the musical equivalent of calendar and postcard pictures: sonatas, fugues, rondos, variations: something they'd heard before and knew how to name and pigeonhole. Schumann liked the Preludes, but then he probably would have liked these pictures, too, and written little character pieces of his own to go with them: "The March to the Red Truck," "The Waltz in the Corncrib," "The Song of the Lonesome Gravestone with Obbligato Wind."

I have scattered these essays with poems by writers I love, the literary ruins and eagle feathers of the Midwest. Bob Firth's pictures are themselves poems—sharp and unexpected images that give us a little glimpse inside ourselves when we look at them—and I thought they deserved some chips of language to stand up alongside them. The old Chinese, too, loved having a poem in the corner of every picture so that they reflected and commented on each other. Often, as with Wang Wei in the Tang Dynasty, poem and picture are the work of the same hand. But this is, for better or worse, the age of specialization; Bob Firth did not hand me a camera, and I did not hand him a pencil.

I'll give you three small poems to try to say what this book is saying, more concisely and elegantly than I am able. I mentioned at the beginning of this preface that a great many people will not much care about the subject of these pictures or essays. Boring, they say. Who wants to look at that old junk? Let's have a sunset over Lake Superior or an interesting shot of moose coupling. Tom Hennen, a poet from Morris, Minnesota, who has spent most of his life working outdoors, has a suggestion that might not cheer up the suspicious reader.

LOVE FOR OTHER THINGS

It's easy to love a deer

But try to pick out insects and scrawny trees

To care about.

Love the puddle of lukewarm water

From last week's rain.

Leave the mountains alone for now.

Also the clear lakes surrounded by pines.

People are already lined up to admire them.

Get close to the things that slide away in the dark.

Think of the frost

That will crack our bones eventually.

Be grateful even for the boredom

That sometimes seems to involve the whole world.

Sometimes just the grass.

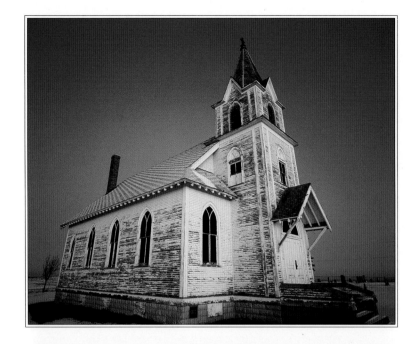

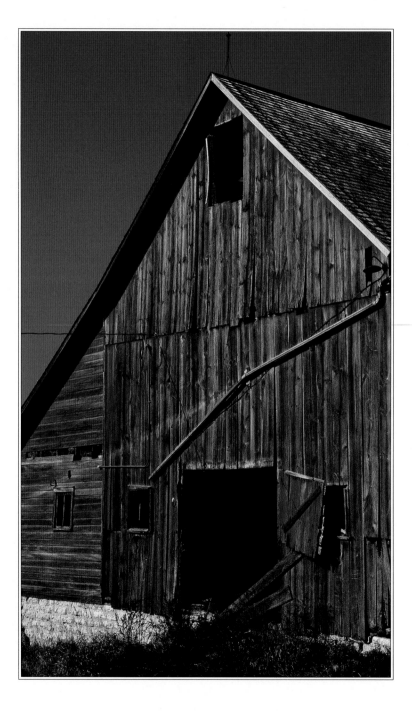

Let your eye amble through the images in this book. It's clear how much Bob Firth loves "other things."

One of my jobs in this book is to put people back in the landscape, to remind these pictures of the world of language and history, still other "other things." Mark Vinz, a Red River Valley man, imagines a postcard arriving from a failed homestead that might look like any place in a Bob Firth photograph.

HOMESTEADER

Somewhere fast trains
howl to each other
through the night valleys.
I dream of them now,
and horses
wild in upland meadows—
moonlight horses
gentle as an old man's tears.

Come visit me—
trains don't stop here anymore,
the mailbox is filling up with snow,
all the fences have been down for years.

This book extends the same invitation: "Come visit me." Human beings lived here, and still do, in their own way.

Finally, pictures of ruined places cannot avoid reminding us of the same process in our own bodies. There is no false cheerfulness in these pictures, and I hope not in the essays either. These images are for psychic grownups. This tiny poem by David Ignatow asks the same question as the old red truck, the cracked window, and the fallen-down barn.

I wish I understood the beauty
in leaves falling. To whom
are we beautiful
as we go?

Bob Firth saw some beauty in the going, and I hope you too find some in this book.

How to Take a Walk

Middle age and fat have driven me to take morning strolls around Minneota, my home town of 1,407 souls. Minneota is about twenty miles from the South Dakota border as the crow flies. It is 112 years old this year in 1993.

What scenery can a stroller look at as he moves through Minneota in the cool damp hour after a July dawn? Considered from one angle, not much. It's about a mile from one end of town to the other—in all directions. Vegetation? This is the northern plains, not good country for trees or flowers: a short growing season, blistering heat, violent wind, and quixotic frosts that Emily Dickinson, though not a Minnesotan, well understood.

> *Apparently with no surprise*
> *To any happy Flower*
> *The Frost beheads it at its play—*
> *In accidental power.*
> *The blond Assassin passes on—*
> *The Sun proceeds unmoved*
> *To measure off another Day*
> *For an Approving God.*

Around the turn of the century, the pioneer town planners must have decided to beautify Minneota by lining all the streets and parks with a thousand boulevard elms. When I was a boy, in the fifties, the now-matured trees arched eighty or ninety feet over the streets, forming a cool green tunnel against the sun and wind. But now, in 1993, the prairie sky is back above town, providing different scenery: thunderheads, northern lights, dusty surreal sunsets. The wind is back too, moving where it pleases through the streets, with neither tall branches nor windmills giving it something else to do. The Dutch Elm Beetle arrived in the sixties, and in ten years finished off all the elms.

Meanwhile, many of the native cottonwoods and boxelders that once lined the Yellow Medicine River were summarily executed by Minneotans who didn't like dirty or misshapen trees. We wanted urban trees, European trees, elegant trees, trees with style and grace and pedigree, trees with a history, even if it is not ours.

We are a new place, hardly a century old, with no grand history or tradition to give us weight and confidence. We borrowed almost everything: our trees, garden flowers and vegetables, farm crops, domestic animals, architecture, institutions, and probably most of our ideas and our sense of ourselves as humans. We even borrowed the only language any of us speak any more—English. Most Minneotans arrived without a word of English, and in the course of learning it over a generation or two, scrapped the old language behind the grove in the junk pile with the rusted machinery parts, two-by-fours full of nails, unwanted field stones left by the glacier. We don't trust what little history we have accumulated in Minneota. In this, we resemble our fellow Americans.

But scenery is not only trees, not only unimproved nature—if such a thing exists outside the world of imagination and desire. Humans too have done something, left interesting tracks, even in Minnesota.

As I circle the town this July morning, I look up. Below the scudding clouds and above both the remaining live trees and the elm

corpses waiting for interment, Minneota has a sort of a skyline. No Chicago or Hong Kong to be sure, but a little height to lift the spirits nonetheless. Here are a gleaming steel water tower that announces the town name, two Lutheran spires to the south and east and a Catholic one to the northwest. The 120-foot white concrete grain elevator rises over them all, the monolith that explains why there's a town here in the first place. Local patriots have climbed to the top by dark to inscribe the concrete with a proud message in bold blue paint: #1. Like every picture that you take in your mind's eye, much less with a camera, this one can be understood in at least two, three, or fifty ways. #1 is the prime and largest of what were once four cooperative grain elevators; locals, on the other hand, understand #1 as a reminder that Minneota was for three years running Minnesota Class C football champions; a philosopher might see #1 yet another way—that Minneota, Minnesota, is the number one Minneota, Minnesota, in the universe, the incarnate Platonic form of itself, all other Minneotas being only timid shallow imitations. An artist might see a great white rectangle topped by a smaller one with metal spouts descending from its sides at interesting angles. The photographer's eye might calculate the massive shadow that monolith intends to cast as the July sun passes overhead. The businessman asks: "Is it full? And what is the price of grain?" But that is the invisible world, whose existence I can only hypothesize as I stroll on a damp July morning. To stroll is to be engaged with the visible.

I left Minneota thirty-one years ago and though I now live here again, the houses I pass on my morning stroll are full of ghosts. Every house is inhabited in my imagination by whoever lived there in say, 1957, the year of the famous Chevy.

There's old Harry, the banker, in dignified brick. There's the chicken magnate, Doc Kerr's house with its hooded awnings. There's the old Josephson house, where Elvira and Victor's father died before I was born, with its grand colonnaded veranda. There's Einar Hallgrimsson's little cottage with its floor-to-ceiling bookshelves. There's Frank and Frida's house where the stamp club met with their perforation gauges and tweezers. There's where Bolga and Sophie made Icelandic pancakes every Sunday morning. There's old Deaf Torgesen's shack. (Old Deaf's nickname was Spring Creek, for his home township.) There's the house of Honore Locy, the ice man whose half-Belgian malapropisms were worthy of Casey Stengel. There's where Uncle Avy's shack used to be before they tore it down. There's where the Norwegian parsonage stood before they moved it. There's where the Round-Up Pool Hall sat, right next to Domenic's building where old Fred had his barber shop.

No one in the rest of America has any idea what I'm talking about; neither do most Minneotans, particularly those under forty or those who moved here from gentler places. In another sense, you, dear reader, know all these people. You recognize the interiors of all these houses. You were present for stamp club and pancakes and tales of the chicken business. You got a haircut from old Fred, you watched Camille and Leonard shoot billiards in the Round-Up, and I was present in your house at Christmas, watching Uncle Albert snore. I ate the bitter herbs of Passover with Auntie Rachel.

Your life in America is neither so exotic nor peculiar as you imagine, whether you grew up in little Minneota by another name, or in a city apartment, or on a cattle ranch on the high plains. We share at least part of a history, part of a culture, and what I think, anyway, is a normal and universal habit of mind. After a certain point, we navigate through our lives by signposts from the dead with the help of ghosts. At any rate, it's the way I find my way around Minneota on strolls on damp July mornings.

Though Minneota is, as American places go, stable, even conservative, almost no house still has the same names inside it that it

had in 1957. I have almost no idea who lives in them now. When my neighbors give me directions, it goes like this: We live two houses east of the old school, torn down in 1957, in the Werpy house, all the Werpys gone since the sixties. I navigate by landmarks long since gone: Drive two miles north where the Gudmundson place used to be. Instead of buildings and a grove, the farmstead is now a soybean field with a majestic rock pile sitting next to it. Almost no one ever moves rock piles; they are the still point in a turning world.

The domestic architecture I pass is full of ghosts too. Our ancestors lived uncertainly on these vast plains. There was enough fear in weather, poverty and a new language without the burden of inventing a new architecture that reflected the terrifying flat emptiness of this landscape. Here are Victorian gingerbread towers and cupolas, invitations for tornadoes to lift them off; here are big open porches with fake Greek columns, invitations for mosquitoes to torture the porch sitters; here are Cape Cod clapboard and shingles, no ocean for thousands of miles; here's a fifties suburban bungalow, no center city for two hundred miles. Here is a picture window facing a dusty street, while a blank wall and a back door face a garden of irises and tulips and a busy goldfinch feeder. Here's an old white prairie box sagging on its fieldstone foundation, paint peeling off the boards, a jungle of hollyhocks hiding a front porch stuffed to its broken screen door with newspapers, empty coffee cans, scrap lumber, broken furniture, stoves and iceboxes—a village rock pile without the rocks. It's probably guarded by a platoon of underfed cats. An eccentric, a pack rat, a hidden grief disguised as parsimony must live here. Next door is a neat bungalow with a bathtub virgin in the garden—white plaster and baby blue painted porcelain. A pious widow must live here. Here's a fleet of junked cars on the edge of town, a field of rust and salvageable auto parts, Fords and Dodges that will drive no further.

At town's edge, my memory stops. Here are the golf course, the new subdivision, brick-fronted villas with electric garage doors; this is the pride of Minneota by whatever name you call it. "It's all new in through here . . . ," says the local tour guide driving you around slowly in his Buick. That sentence is always accompanied by a gesture, a sort of slow sweeping of the forearm, fingers extended past the new mall, the new development, the new X-Mart by whatever name, the new windowless high school that looks like a cross between a security prison and a chemical factory, the new nursing home shingled with unpainted cedar, the new corn-alcohol plant with its old chicken-house whiff. That armsweep includes not just a half a mile of buildings on the edge of town, but a whole vast stretch of American consciousness. "It's all new in through here" is not a description, but a code, a badge of honor, a way we have chosen to inhabit and populate our landscape—both interior and exterior.

We Americans still don't quite know what to do about history. Our fondest national hope seems to be that it not repeat itself in any form. We are always a little disingenuously surprised when it does: one more depression, one more round of religious fervor, one more little war that gets too big for its britches. We still haven't quite figured out how we really are connected to Europe, much less Asia, Africa, or our own Latin neighbors to the south, much less to our own history of events.

Yet, we have an uneasy conscience about this. We are impressed by the age and grandeur of foreign ruins, and a little defensive about our own. We think we ought to pickle more of our past and make a theme park out of it. Neglecting the fact that everybody's grandfather, without distinction of race, creed, or gender, was a washout, we want to buy a coat of arms, grow some ethnic pride, and set out a few heirlooms in the landscape for passersby to admire.

The German writer Goethe early in the nineteenth century, a generation before America had begun to hatch a literature that mattered to the world, gave the United States some odd counsel.

DEN VEREINIGTEN STAATEN

Amerika, du hast es besser
Als unser Kontinent, das alte,
Hast keine verfallene Schlösser
Und keine Basalte,
Dich Stört nicht im Innern
Zu lebendiger Zeit,
Unnutzes Erinnern
Und vergeblicher Streit.

Benutzt die Gegenwart mit Glück!
Und wenn nun eure Kinder dichten,
Bewahre sie ein gut Geschick
Vor Ritter-, Räuber-
und Gespenstergeschichten.

THE UNITED STATES

America, you are luckier
Than this old continent of ours;
You have no ruined castles
And no volcanic earth.
You do not suffer
In hours of intensity
From futile memories
And pointless battles.

Concentrate on the present joyfully!
And when your children write books
May a good destiny keep them
From knight, robber, and ghost-
stories.

—translated by Robert Bly

Give up history! Yes! What good has it ever done Europe? What we read in the daily newspaper about the Balkans sounds like a rerun newsreel of 1914—or for that matter 1614 or 1314. German skinheads beat up blackhaired people and paint swastikas to mark their territory. The Russians search for unmurdered relatives of the Romanovs to lead them out of chaos. The Muslims and the Crusaders still fight it out shrine-to-shrine in the ghost-haunted streets of Jerusalem. And on and on and on . . .

Goethe meant well, but like most Europeans he underestimated the staying power of history in the New World. We can't start over here and avoid falling into the old traps. We never could, though for a while we fooled ourselves.

We can make something different—sometimes something fine and lovely and sane and we have now and then, but not without growing a consciousness. What you see on a morning walk around Minneota has stringers going back thousands of years. We don't quite have ruined castles, but we have junked cars and deserted farmsteads, and sometimes they all speak the same language, preach the same sermon down to the new generations. Sometimes also they share romantic charm and visual elegance, but we must not let it carry us away. That is nostalgia: a black and treacherous pit almost impossible for human beings to climb out from.

The German phrase, here translated as "no volcanic earth," is "keine Basalte." I like "basalt" better. It is heavy, black, scientific, a hard fact, something you find in rock piles; but like any fact, once you have acknowledged its presence, you can move around it, examine it, see what it's got to say for itself. The basalt of history sits under Minneota, as it does under your own house.

I think I'd translate "Benützt die Gegenwart mit Glück!" as "It's all new in through here, and we're damn proud of it," with a tag end of "Have a nice day." What you hold in your hand is a book of pictures of ruins, ghosts of your own history, failures, decomposing buildings and machines, waste and detritus of a progressive mercantile culture that believed in growth, progress, neatness, and compulsive up-to-dateness. What you now read is a series of half-ironic, half-cranky and bad-tempered essays praising things that went wrong, machines that stopped running, buildings that fell down and windows that cracked and melted. The photographer's argument is: Look at these things; here, too, is joy. The writer's argument is: Leave them alone and let them die in peace; they carry our history on their shoulders and have not lost the power to delight and teach us, sometimes even to tell us jokes and make us weep. "It's all new in through here" can only describe a world without memory, therefore without intelligence and humanity.

"Concentrate on the present joyfully" will land you in more wars, depressions, and catastrophes, both personal and public, than you can well imagine.

Heiner Müller, a writer from the former East Germany, is less cheerful than Goethe and has different advice for Americans. He's paid attention to the 160 years of history since Goethe's death. In talking about our modern mania to legislate moral perfection, physical neatness and environmental correctness, he says: "A perfect world is terminal; there is no life without ruins. You can be happy about every dying tree because it proves there is still life. When I eat muesli in the morning, an hour later I want to shoot myself. I'd rather drink gasoline for breakfast."

I'm still out strolling on a damp July morning. I've walked past the "all-new-in-through-here" neighborhood, admired the fine wreck of an old greenhouse with all its windows shot out, circumambulated the grain elevators, inspected a junked '47 Chevy with its green hood bent forever open, passed the newly eyeless brick school, and reached the edge of town where the road curves north and east past farms. Here, walking for no visible reason other than pleasure or the chance to let the mind work, is a dicier matter. The poet Leo Dangel from South Dakota understands this danger and gives us instructions.

HOW TO TAKE A WALK

This is farming country.
The neighbors will believe
you are crazy
if you take a walk
just to think and be alone.
So carry a shotgun
and walk the fence line.
Pretend you are hunting
and your walking will not
arouse suspicion.
But don't forget
to load the shotgun.
They will know
if your gun is empty.
Stop occasionally.
Cock your head and listen
to the doves you never see.
Part the tall weeds
with your hand and inspect
the ground.
Sniff the air as a hunter would.
(That wonderful smell
of sweet clover is a bonus.)
Soon you will forget
the gun in your hands,
but remember, someone
may be watching.
If you hear beating wings
and see the bronze flash
of something flying up,
you will have to shoot it.

But I don't carry a shotgun—only paper, pencils and peppermints. I will have to do my shooting with them. My friend Firth carries a black box on his walks and sometimes hides under a black shroud during long exposures. He has more than once been mistaken for a hunter and driven with rude threats away from a good shot. The thought that goes through an owner's head must go something like this: That man is taking pictures of junk—my junk. If he thinks it worth photographing, then it must be worth money, and can't be junk. Therefore (goes the inexorable logic), he must intend either to steal or vandalize it. It is therefore my American duty to drive him out.

Now I've reached gravel and head north. I cross an old wood bridge over the Yellow Medicine River as it snakes its way east out of town toward Granite Falls, the Mississippi, the Gulf of Mexico, and finally the Gulf Stream. Things travel a long way in this universe if you begin thinking about them. In this wet, gray summer, the brush is dense along the river, the boxelders lush and heavy as magnolias for a change, and the creek full to its banks, proud of its current, with even a little discreet ripple. The first farm north of the river belongs to the Gudmundsons, two Icelandic brothers and a sister, Pete and Staney and Anna, all unmarried, all born in the nineteenth century. The farmstead is empty now, and nothing is "new in through here." Staney is dead, and Anna and Pete are in the nursing home only a mile or two away, thinking in their childhood Icelandic and waiting patiently, both well past ninety. The buildings are old—and old-fashioned—but still neat, orderly, well painted, as if they wanted some twinkly, ancient, Luddite farmer to move back in for a few years with a team of horses and finish out their usefulness before beginning the long decay into rubble.

I stand in the yard for a while, chewing peppermints, smoking, mopping my forehead, looking things over, thinking about the almost thirty years I've known and visited that farmstead. The Gudmundsons

This conversation took place in 1990. Eighty-seven years is, indeed, a little thin to begin claiming a place as home. I think Staney understood history and basalt and ruined castles. Being "from here" requires a consciousness of the ghosts in a landscape; it requires some leavings to remind us; it requires us to be alert to what we see when we take our walks over the earth, whether we bring along a black box with a lens, a shotgun, or a notebook. If we don't see what is in front of us, we will never manage, either as private humans or as a culture, to be *from* anywhere at all.

were the last farmers around Minneota to practice old-fashioned corn picking. They still produced cobs. My cousin, who burns cobs in his cook stove, went out to get a load and to visit the Gudmundsons. While he was loading his cobs in a truck, he asked Staney why the Gudmundsons happened to farm so far from other settlements of Icelanders in the neighborhood. Staney meditated for a second:

"We're not really *from* here, you know."

"You're not?" exclaimed my cousin, who had known them in the same place for almost sixty years.

"Dad homesteaded in Lincoln County. We only moved here in 1903."

Paint: A Moral Question

When weathered barn boards became fashionable in suburban dens, some farmers began meticulously disassembling and peddling what would otherwise have been left to the natural process of architectural composting. The more beaten up by blizzards and hailstorms and blistered and baked by sun, the more charmingly rural in a Wayzata breakfast nook or fireside cranny. "It's so—country!" the neighbors might remark over cocktails and canapés. Few real farm kitchens or parlors were ever paneled with gray boards from the grove or from the old chicken house. Real farms wanted new plaster or sheet rock covered with floral wallpaper from Sears.

Fresh paint in the right color, assumed in my boyhood, and probably still, the power of moral virtue. It was as if God had said, "Let the house be white and the barn red, and go to the hardware store every couple of years where new cans of paint can be bought for cash. Do this in remembrance of me . . ." And so it was. A farmer or a small-town home or store owner who neglected his buildings was thought by his neighbors to have taken either to drink, book reading, pure sloth or probably all three interlocked.

I once did some oral history in an almost entirely Swedish small town just north of Saint Paul. The new nursing home was a handsome building, sided with cedar, and left to weather. The still tan and aromatic shingles had only begun their journey toward gray. A bunch of old fellows sat outside on the front patio each day, parked their wheelchairs, walkers, and canes, took the sun, smoked, chewed snoose and spat, commenting on the general state of things in their still Swedish-accented voices. One continual object of their Copenhagen-flavored scorn was their new and last home. "Damn shame . . . you'd think they couldn't afford paint . . . look at that across the field! Arvid's barn with a fresh coat . . . Arvid's cows deserve better than we do . . ."

We are charmed and amused by their curmudgeonly and unfashionable taste for fresh paint. Look at it from their angle: These old geezers are themselves either immigrants or sons of immigrants. They came from an old socially complicated half-ruined Sweden, poor men with no future in their own home. Sweden, like all Europe, is full of ruins, antiques, ancient churches, country houses, ghosts of history—both glories and failures. That history included no place for these men. They came to Chisago County, the "new" world, to eat, own things themselves, and rise into the realm of the respectable. If a man had worked hard enough to own a barn, he damn well ought to paint it and take care of it. If you sell the cattle, then salvage the good lumber, build a granary, and paint that. The sentimental fashion for rural "charm" was not likely to tempt them. They regarded weathered siding as an economic insult, almost a moral failure.

Whatever the practical farmer's view or the current home-decorating fad, it is artists, particularly photographers and poets, who love weathered boards more than fresh paint. A television station in Saint Paul once asked to do a half-hour filming of one of my essays about rural Minnesota. Despite my prejudice that television is the cardinal liar in American life, I told them to come have a look at

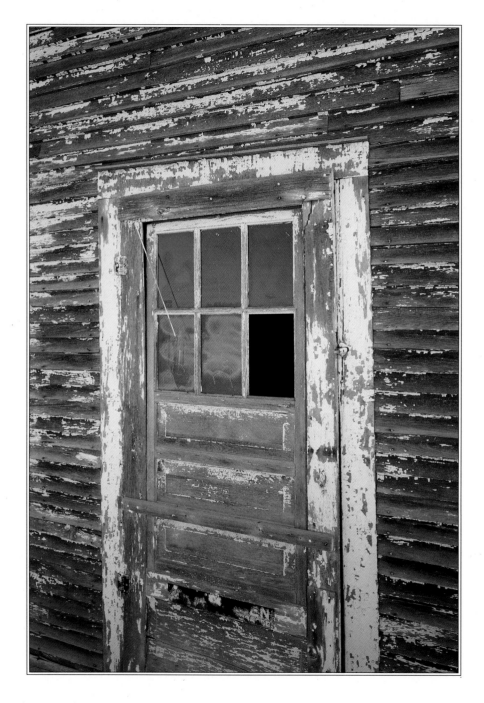

Minneota and take pictures wherever they pleased, even though in the common view of visitors from the Twin Cities there was not much to look at "out here." They arrived, photographed, and to my surprise, were completely charmed by the look of the landscape through the cold glass eye of a television camera. The sky did its best tricks for them, garish mottled sunsets, lowering thunderheads, and one night even outperformed itself by staging simultaneous heat lightning to the south, aurora borealis to the north, and a glittering Milky Way to yoke the two together.

They liked, as Bob Firth does, old schools, silos, elevators, leaning barns, empty granaries, defrocked churches, rusted tractors, and aggressive thistles. The energy-saving windowless high school, the drive-up teller booth on the new bank, or the computer pump at the do-it-yourself-frozen-pizza gas station did not strike them as being good TV. It's probably not good life either, but television is not the instrument to give us that particular news.

One fine June day, we drove through the Lincoln County hills, looking for photo opportunities, when the cameraman spotted a handsomely bleak abandoned farmstead on a rise just off the county road. The grove was gone and the windowless house with its attendant barn and granary had turned gunmetal gray from sun, wind, and storms. A few shards of glass still glistened in the window frames; indoors, mice had eaten their fill and scattered the stuffing from a couch and chair too old and ruined to move. Canadian thistles, buffalo burr, milkweed, and wild oats grew waist high to the cracked foundations, then swished around photogenically in the summer wind. This scene of human failure and natural desolation was a cameraman's piece of cake. For frosting, the sun began sinking to illuminate the gray boards, broken glass, and weeds with a sideways orange glow. The cameraman stayed there a long time, looking happy as he swiveled his

machine to catch light and angles and shadows. The sound woman walked around in earphones, brandishing her microphone, collecting "ambiance" as the TV sorts call it: an environment of noises—wind in grass, crickets, tunes of mourning doves and meadowlarks. Meanwhile, I hid in the car against the mosquitoes, probably reading a French novel about grasping peasants and crooked shopkeepers. I am, after all, as the locals say, "from here."

Later, when I saw the scene on television as the editor imagined it and snipped it into place, I was stunned and half delighted. The old ruined farm was gorgeous, magnificent—eerily beautiful. Add your own string of unmidwestern adjectives. Over it came the sound woman's "ambiance," melancholy Estonian violin music, and my voice reading an essay in praise of failure. While not quite reality, it was a nice piece of work—a stab at greater truth telling than commercials or political speeches provide.

Curiously, people began calling after the broadcast to compliment me on the handsomeness of the landscape—as if writers invented what they described!—but also to offer pity and consolation that my ancestral farm should be a dismal and attractively romantic ruin, a sort of rural midwestern "House of Usher." "It must sadden you to go out there," they'd say. "That's not my father's farm!" I huffed back. "His farm now belongs to good new farmers who have pulled down the shabby old chicken house, put up a new sheet-metal shed, and planted a decent grove. It's a going farm—depending, as always, on interest rates and the price of grain. I have no idea who the hell lived in that old shack in Lincoln County. Nobody I know!"

So much for the connection between art and life. There is a kind of essential truth in those old weathered boards, their condition of spiritual and actual paintlessness, their color stripped away by age, history, economics, nature. They show us part of ourselves not visible

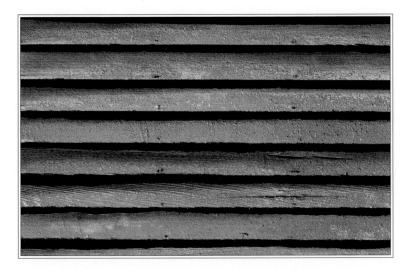

next to the new windowless, sheet-metal prefab life of the moment, a part not always cheerful and comfortable to think about. Sometimes they show us unexpected joy. Poets, like photographers, pass by the new subdivision without a single metaphorical quivering of their pencils, but an old board that has been battered and beautified by its history has probably got something valuable for human beings lying under it. Robert Bly, my neighbor in southwestern Minnesota, noticed these old boards on his Madison, Minnesota, farmstead.

OLD BOARDS

I

I love to see boards lying on the ground in early spring:
The ground beneath them is wet and muddy—
Perhaps covered with chicken tracks—
And they are dry and eternal.

II

This is the wood one sees on the decks of ocean ships,
Wood that carries us far from land,
With a dryness of something used for simple tasks,
Like a horse's tail.

III

This wood is like a man who has a simple life,
Living through the spring and winter on the ship of his own desire.
He sits on dry wood surrounded by half-melted snow
As the rooster walks away springily over the dampened hay.

If you try to build the ship of your desire out of sheet metal, I predict it won't sail far.

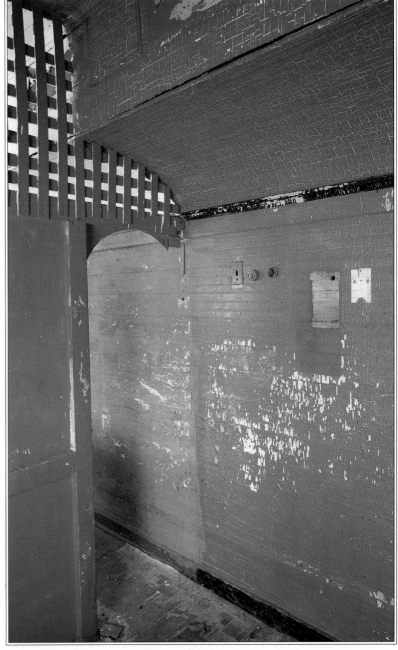

The Music of Light in Old Windows

I grew up sleeping in the northwest room in the new part of an old farmhouse north of Minneota. My grandfather built the "old" part in about 1883 when he homesteaded, but when his third child arrived in 1900, he celebrated the new century by adding a wing. By the time I began sleeping there, in the late forties, the glass in the single window was almost a half century old. It faced west, looking out on the upper branches of one gnarled old boxelder tree whose bare twigs scratched the window when blizzards arrived from the Rockies a few thousand miles west. These blizzards were invariably accompanied by the locally famous wind, the Alberta Clipper, that rattled the poor loose old window in the frame, banging the glass with everything it carried in its fists: horizontal handfuls of snow, pebbles, grit, ice pellets. It's a wonder either the window, the bent weedy tree, or the boy sleeping under his pile of quilts behind that frail protection survived these brisk onslaughts. I remember watching the water in the glass by my bedside slowly freezing into ice, a little grateful that my grandfather had not decided to add a north window too in that small room. The west provided quite enough fresh air, scenic grandeur and excitement. Whatever comes from the north in January, for instance, is best kept private and invisible.

In winter, though, when the window wasn't sheathed in ice, I saw west through the bare branches of the grove to the glacial ridge of hills and gullies many miles away that signaled the beginning of South Dakota. By summer, my view shrank to leaves. Now the long humid sunsets seemed likely to melt that poor window and let the wet heat drown me in my bed. Mosquitoes, flies, moths, June bugs, and bees dive-bombed the window, sometimes doing a kamikaze splat into the old glass on their way to try to keep me company. I had a polka-dot view of my private boxelder through a sort of translucent insect graveyard.

It was a normal boyhood in a farmhouse on the northern prairie, and I remark on it only to express my gratitude to that window which gave me both pleasure and protection. It was my first eye into the great space of America to the west, and sometimes into the gleaming eye of the horned owl who sat in the branches just outside the window, watching for foolish rabbits, gophers, and mice, then hooting me sweetly to sleep.

The glass in that half-century-old window suffered for me. Like a human being who endures almost a century of bludgeoning by nature and experience, glass shows its age. Glass also resembles us in that it is not a finished thing. Whatever happens to it alters it. The light this year never looks quite the same as the light that passed through last year, or intends to travel through next year, should the glass live through winter.

Glass is always in transit to something else. It is not a thing, but a condition, a state of being. Sometimes, looking through old church windows, or the half broken shards left in a deserted farmhouse, I think it is a consciousness, but then I am a transcendentalist (or an American, if there is a difference), and Americans entertain such ideas now and then.

But any trip into the world of spirit starts, as Emerson reminded us, with the world of fact. The first fact about glass is its recipe: sand, soda, and fire. In the West, we credit the discovery to the

Mesopotamians, who probably cooked the first glass somewhere in the neighborhood of our recent American bombing raids. I have a suspicion that the Chinese probably beat the Mesopotamians to the punch, but whoever did it did well. Glass shares with other human triumphs the elegance of simplicity, a wonder always apparent if we could only have thought of it.

Beyond the recipe and the pleasure, I knew nothing of glass, so I went to a scientist—a colleague of mine at the college where I teach—a chemist, a glassblower, and an enthusiast for nature and intelligence. Ed Carberry is a small wiry man, full of energy, whose face lights up and begins moving the moment the chemistry of glass comes up in talk. Thinking of the wavery light I loved so much in the windows of old farmhouses, I asked Ed if glass ages. Ed delivered a little lecture on glass, darting around my office, picking up ashtrays and empty pop bottles for visual aids, pointing to a jumbled heap of books.

If glass looks uniform, it's new; if not, not. Old glass is invariably full of air bubbles, pieces of undissolved sand, imperfections. Glass is not a solid at all (so much for the world of appearances, and its happy tricks on us), but a supercooled liquid, a flowing, continuously in motion, whatever our eye might perceive. Glass begins life in an amorphous state; its evolution is to crystallize. What does this mean?

Amorphousness in nature is disorder, something without pattern. Ed points to a jumbled heap of books. As glass ages, it develops pattern and order—it crystallizes. Ed points to an orderly row of alphabetically organized books sitting like obedient soldiers in a neat line on their shelf. Nature, like a severe great-aunt, intends to damn well crystallize that glass, to shape it up and make something of it. Paradoxically, the strength of glass lies in its amorphousness—its lack of uniformity and pattern. Glass that has been crystallized by fire or age is brittle, weak, ready to shatter at the slightest touch. Remember Aunt Mabel's warning

not to touch her antique figurine, and your horror when at the tenderest of feathery touches the poor figurine shattered and collapsed, and with it, any chance you had of being remembered fondly in Aunt Mabel's will. For once, you were not morally culpable; crystallization simply triumphed over amorphousness, and you were an innocent instrument of extreme unction for the figure. Forgive yourself; something like that process is happening inside your own body, too.

Glass also resembles your body in that everything it touches changes it: rain, dust, carbon dioxide, other chemicals and pollutants in the air, heat and cold. Old buried bottles turn mottled and frosty; the soil eats at them, and leaves them pocked and uneven. You, too. Every time you drink, you take a little of the glass with you along with the whiskey. If, like a Russian, you hurl the glass at the fireplace, it breaks not in straight chunks but with curved surfaces. It is not done crystallizing yet. Neither are you. Glass, born in fire, dies by fire, too.

By now, Ed and I were hurling metaphors back and forth like glass blocks. He had a class to teach, and as he ducked out of my office, looked wistfully back at the shelves of poetry. "Science is nothing without imagination," he said, a little sadly, but then perking up, added, "poetry is nothing without fact." A wise man . . . There is much to be learned about the universe by blowing glass.

Yet, having outfoxed nature by melting sand and soda, we have now, thousands of years later, begun to dishonor our human inventiveness by disinventing the window. The saddest building in a small town is an old neo-gothic school with its eyes sewn shut. When the Arabs raised the price of fuel oil in the seventies, a madness disguised as practical thrift infected Minnesotans and other Americans. They bricked up their grand old rattley windows to save money, and in so doing robbed their children of light. Architects without souls were even found to build new schools blind from birth—bare concrete walls

without a window. Who needs air and light? Surely not human beings.

I have taught for many years in such a school building. The rooms inside are dead, and dead things prosper there. Intelligence and a lively soul want light through glass, and visible wind and weather.

An old wrecked farmhouse, on the other hand, is full of life even though no one has lived in it for years. These farmhouses punctuate the countryside. "Eyesores," intones the practical voice. "Tear them down, and plant another acre of corn to be cooked into alcohol for your gas tank." Yet that part of our communal soul that includes both the artist and the historian loves old windows and the buildings where they live.

Perhaps it is not windows we love so much as light, and the window becomes the instrument by which light plays on us and in us. An old window is like an old pump organ or an old violin. You can't play heavy metal, electric disco, or minimalist doodling on it, but there is still music in it that sings to us. We don't trade in Palestrina or Bach because we can't plug them in, and we don't send Byrd or Handel to the junk pile because their noises are not practical, economical, and state-of-the-art-cutting-edge-bottom-line technology. Even if the reeds inside the old pump organ wheeze a little or there is a tiny crack in the bridge of the violin, we listen to the music of their old age—if we have any sense or soul. We have a little wheezing and a few tiny cracks inside us, too.

I'll give you three places where the music of light through old windows has worked on me. They are intended to remind you of the places where it has worked inside you.

Southwest of Minneota, in Lincoln County, the Polish Catholics and the Icelandic Lutherans built churches a couple of miles apart. The Poles flourished and grew, the Icelanders withered and closed their doors, but the light inside both churches is simultaneously a wonder and a lesson in theology. The Polish church is vast and airy, flooded

with dark light coming in behind the nineteenth-century stained glass. The windows are full of saints dressed in richly colored robes: purple, olive, burgundy, deep brown and ocher. Below the saints are dedications in Polish, mysterious words without vowels, backlit by prairie sun. My favorite is Saint George looking smug in his snug helmet, sword thrown jauntily over his shoulder, fresh dragon blood reddening the blade, the reptile's green horny tail under his boot. At sunset, St. George lights up

more brilliantly than a Las Vegas casino sign. In that church, the light is medieval. It is old Catholic light. It has little to do with the twentieth century or logic or agribusiness or picture tubes or voice mail. That light has monks singing inside it.

A few miles east, the Icelanders saved money by not choosing stained glass—either that or they wanted the clear Protestant light of plain pale gold opaque windows that burnished the oak carpentry, but cast no images. Only pure light, reformed light, light saved by grace alone and not by works. The white frame, now ramshackle church is bare, severe, elegant in its plain no-nonsense directness. This was a room to think in—to listen to the wind and remember dead relatives mouldering a few feet away in the graveyard. I always had the feeling as a boy that whatever formal words Icelanders said in church, most of them were none too sure that there was, in fact, a next life outside the inexorable chemistry of matter. So they designed light for the mind to work by; the heart would have to move west or bide its time. Jefferson would have liked this skeptical, Deist, benevolent light; it was the eighteenth-century light that organized America.

The Icelandic church is in bad repair, in danger of disappearing. A couple of the pale windows are already cracked out, replaced by a splintery plywood eyepatch. I would miss the light in either of those two churches. By themselves, they are incomplete; together, they include the world.

I went to college in St. Peter, Minnesota, a river town and one of the oldest settled places in the state. The town itself was a showcase of grand old mansions from before the Civil War, and the Minnesota River Valley was well populated by ghosts of failed towns and farms, places missed by the railroad or done in by drought, flood, or bank failure. Ottawa, an almost ghost town on the east side of the river, was my favorite hunting ground for romantic ruins. Driving one day down

a pot-holey road through deep woods, I discovered a ruined stone farmhouse surrounded by piles of junk. In my boyish imagination it was a house straight from Brontë country. In fact, it was only a failed farm from the 1860s, half burned out, half simply left to compost back into the valley muck. The window frames were set in arched masonry, most of the windows partly broken out, weeds and seedlings growing up in and around them. But that old glass, whether from fire, age or both,

bent the soft green light so that you looked at the ruined stone walls as if from under the sea—some magical sunken castle inhabited by mermaids with silky black hair. For a farm boy going to a Lutheran college at the end of the fifties, that light and those ruins were a fine escape from the world of John Foster Dulles, J. Edgar Hoover, and "get a job." That Ottawa ruin, hardly peculiar, exists within a mile or two of your own house. Think twice about bulldozing it and putting up a windowless high school. Something necessary for human beings can be seen only by the bent green light through those old windows.

The most famous, probably the most beautiful, building in Minnesota stands not in Minneapolis or Saint Paul, but in Owatonna, a small town on the southern prairies. Louis Sullivan, Frank Lloyd Wright's mentor, and very likely America's most imaginative and original architect, was down on his luck after the turn of the century. His career petered out and he found himself reduced to taking commissions for small town banks. When the Owatonna banker hired him in 1906, he put everything he knew about light and space into a moderate-sized brick box in the middle of nowhere. I had heard of this famous bank since boyhood, but saw it for the first time only a few years ago. I walked inside during a Sunday winter sunset, the bank empty and silent. I am a garrulous, even a glib man, but for a minute after I felt the light in that room, language deserted me. The windows are huge arches of green glass, a multicolored skylight above. The elegant terra cotta electroliers, the bas relief decorations, the old varnish on the wood, all glowed as if lit from inside. I had not understood until then that architecture has little or nothing to do with joints, foundations, plumbing, or square feet of space; its real business is with the imagination of light. Those old windows and skylights make a room expensive to heat and maintain. They waste space that could be used for business. Yet, as in any old farmhouse or barn or high school or church,

those windows are the whole point. Miss it, and you miss everything—eventually even your own inner life.

The window connects human beings and nature. No surprise that photographers love glass—beginning with their own lenses, the artificial eye that drinks light and records it on glass or tin plates or plastic to show us what our own universe looks like. No surprise, either, that they love taking pictures of old windows, a labyrinth of glass filled with light dancing back and forth between lens, window, eye, and sky.

I think I knew, even as a boy lying in the northwest room of the farmhouse my grandfather built, that it wasn't only me looking out at the boxelder tree or at the distant ridge that started the high plains, but it was also something out in all that air and light looking back at the fat, pink boy under his quilts. It is not the smallest marvel of glass that we see both in and out. We can never quite name what looks back at us, but we know it's there.

And God Said: "Let There Be Red"

"Were you born in a barn?" asked your mother in a sardonic voice after discovering one of your messes, or after having to close a door you had left open in your childhood forgetfulness and sloth. "Just like Jesus," a smart comeback, earned you either the back of a hand or a stern command to bring your chaos into civilized order.

Actually, if your mother thought about that question, and if you were born on a normal farm, she would have realized that it was not an insult at all. The barn, most frequently, was larger, cleaner, better appointed, sometimes warmer, and in its architecture, more elegant than your house. It was all right for human beings to be cramped, uncomfortable, and cold, but cattle, horses, and pigs deserved better, and hay needed to stay drier than children.

The famous old story by Mary E. Wilkins Freeman, "The Revolt of Mother," set in New England, is a sort of prefeminist fable. It could as well have been set in the Midwest. Mother's behavior, rather than making a political statement, is a touchstone of simple rationality. Maybe that's the function of true political gestures: to restore fellow citizens to the light of reason. Father, after promising for too many years to build a new house to replace the cramped wreck in which mother has raised their children almost to adulthood, cannot resist the temptation to build a new barn instead in order to expand his livestock herd. He builds a fine new barn, goes off to dicker for more cattle, and brings home his new stock, only to find that Mother moved into the new barn, stove, four-poster bed, crystal punchbowl, oak rocker, and all—the whole catastrophe. She has no intention of moving back, so the poor livestock have to make do with the old house.

It's a fine comic reversal, so long as you are of Mother's party. Most of my boyhood neighbors in Swede Prairie township would have tried to figure out how to get Mother up to the Cities for a few days to calm her down, so that they could discreetly move her back where she belonged. Then they could proceed to run that silage auger into the east side and buy ten more head.

In the Cities, Father puts on his necktie, snaps shut his briefcase, and goes off in his Volvo every morning to battle the dragon of freeway traffic before doing his daily hunting and gathering at a desk under fluorescent lights in a glass and iron box. He surfaces again into the domestic world after dark, if golf or late meetings have not distracted him on the way home. So goes the old cliché of the American salary man. Like all clichés, it's about half true.

In the other part of this cliché, Mother stays at home in a fine suburban house, vacuuming carpets, dusting bric-a-brac, ferrying daughter to dance class, son to Little League, then stopping at the mall to price new sofas, sideboards, and decorator prints of charming rural scenes before station wagoning back down the cul-de-sac to make ginger cookies and pot roast. The metaphor behind this imaginary family, of course, is that the urban domestic world and the world of business and affairs are invisible to each other, separated by sharp demarcations of space and habit. This cliché, mostly true, is a primary distinction between urban and rural life.

On a farm, business and domesticity face each other across a narrow yard with iron and intractable faces. They deal with each other, mix, negotiate, interpenetrate, not always gladly, but always necessarily.

One sees what the other does at every moment of every day in every season. What is taken from one world is received by the other. These two worlds are a balance scale with manure and a yard light between them. If a new truckload of feeder cattle weights one end, the other rises until a new washing machine or living room suite brings back the balance. The idea of a farm as a happy unity painted by Norman Rockwell is the purest nonsense. The house and the barn are a pair of contraries, often in silent war with one another, at their best in a state of creative tension. The barn is the world of business and affairs. Historically and practically, it wins.

If you drive by almost any deserted farmstead, notice that the barn has outlasted the house. It was better built and better maintained through most of its history. Often a barn went on giving useful service, storing hay, livestock, machinery, long after the house turned into a rest home for mice and pigeons, or a practice target for marauding teenage boys. By the time the barn developed its elegant lean, a harbinger of its end, the house usually suffered a terminal illness and was either cremated or bulldozed into the rock pile.

The only inflexible rule of barn architecture was red—no other color would do. A barn was something like Henry Ford's description of customer options on the Model T. He would make one for you in any color you wanted so long as it was black. Beyond red, barn design provided more avenues for the expression of whimsy, creativity, and newfangled fashion than a house. The gaiety of cupolas; the imaginative trim on a hay barn door; the haughtiness of weather vanes and lightning rods; the sense of height and soaring in a steeply pitched roof; the shape of the barn itself: rectangle, hexagon, circle; the grand size that proclaimed wealth and power; the meticulous stone masonry of the foundation; the ingenious trapdoors and feeding chutes; the narrow medieval stairs into the hay mow; the vaulted cathedral ceilings to keep the alfalfa safe and dry; the nooks and crannies where cats slept between their shifts savaging barn rats and giving apoplexy to pigeons; the imperial rows of orderly stanchions for milk cows; the grand canal of the gutter . . . There was poetry in most barns, but only expository prose in the house. Mrs. Wilkins' revolting mother probably meant to make her children into artists by moving them into the new barn. It's an odd paradox (but then what paradox isn't?) that the world of practical business fed the soul while the house fed the body its everyday hot dish and watery coffee.

Some of the grandest lines of American literature were born in a barn. Long Island was still rural when Walt Whitman grew up there in the 1820s, and he remembered the barns of his own childhood with delight in "Song of Myself."

The big doors of the country barn stand open and ready,
The dried grass of the harvest-time loads the slow-drawn wagon,
The clear light plays on the brown gray and green intertinged,
The armfuls are pack'd to the sagging mow.

I am there, I help, I came stretch'd atop of the load,
I felt its soft jolts, one leg reclined on the other,
I jump from the cross-beams and seize the clover and timothy,
And roll head over heels and tangle my hair full of wisps.

If you read those last two lines aloud, you might be tempted to do somersaults all over your living room. Does it surprise you that children love hay barns more than churches, school rooms or their own cramped houses?

As a grown man Whitman thought not of the excitement of barns, but of their calm and loveliness, and what could be seen looking out from them.

A FARM PICTURE

Through the ample open door of the peaceful country barn,
A sunlit pasture field with cattle and horses feeding,
And haze and vista, and the far horizon fading away.

The little scene he paints has been photographed on farm co-op calendars for a long time now, and though a visual cliché, has not lost its power to charm and take us away for a few seconds from the frenzy of our noisy century.

The most famous barn around Minneota when I was a boy belonged to my eccentric cousins, Victor and Elvira Josephson, twins, university educated, the last living children of their wealthy father. They read books, raised an army of cats, never married, and built round buildings. The barn went up around 1910, an experimental design from the University of Minnesota Agriculture Extension, a pre–World War I state-of-the-art cow, horse, and hay house. It sat surrounded by a fine grove next to the Yellow Medicine River, almost invisible from the county road, only the top of the shingled dome and a gleaming cupola peeking above the trees.

Victor and Elvira died a month apart in the mid-sixties. The house burned the night after the sale. The new farmers who bought the land plowed straight up to the river, leaving the round barn for the first time in its history fully exposed to marauding photographers. They rose to the bait with their cameras, and for about fifteen years Kodak made a fortune, developing all-season photographs of that splendid barn.

But no livestock lived there any more: The round barn, since it served no practical purpose, was left to the mercy of weather and decay. The shingles on the vast, steeply curved roof slid off as they rotted randomly, leaving maybe a hundred holes of light forty feet above your head. The effect, like a low sky full of star points, was more romantic

and lovely in its dying than it had ever been while still in good repair. The round roof was an acoustical marvel, too. I practiced opera arias there on sunny afternoons. Even a church choir duffer sounded like Caruso after a passionate Italian phrase reverberated around that roof and bounced back onto the bare wood floor, hayless for the first time in its history. A plainsong would have sounded well, too, but somehow seemed culturally misplaced in the barn of Icelandic agnostics.

Not only eyes and ears were charmed by that barn; the nose loved it best of all. Once cattle and horses have eaten and shat and slept, been born and died in a room, the boards smell of them. The smells of old hay, leather, sour milk, dust, cats, petrified manure, cheap pipe tobacco, haunt you forever in old barns. Oddly, almost no one thinks of those smells as decay, sadness, or failure. There are a kind old quilt pulled over your nose on a blizzardy night. Whoever bottled that smell would earn the gratitude of the human race. One sniff might calm an army or almost make a politician truthful.

It was a sensual old barn too. I once fell in love with an Icelandic woman from the old country, and took her there on a fine summer afternoon. This is what happened.

ROUND BARN

She and I go to an old round barn by the river.
The barn is full of the smell of old hay.
Wind whistles through missing shingles in the high dome.
Iron stalls are empty now.
We see hoof prints on black dirt, made by cattle long since dead
and eaten. From a nail she takes down a horse harness, leather
dried and cracked.
"From Iceland," she says, and caresses it.
We walk into the empty hayloft, fifty feet high, shaped like a
cathedral dome. The last sunlight blown into the holes in the dome
by prairie winds shines the floor like a polished ballroom.
I walk under the dome, open my mouth, and sing—an old Italian
song about the lips of Lola the color of cherries.
The sound rolls around the dome and grows.
It comes back to me transformed into horse's neighing.

The barn is gone now, its lumber recycled and its old cattle yard growing rich soybeans. But the countryside wherever you are will still provide a curious old barn or two for you to visit when your life presents you with the need. Old barns are fine places for singing, for contemplation, for love. If, in old age, you grow crotchety and awkward, and some snarly young attendant snaps at you, "Were you born in a barn?" smile sweetly and answer, "Yes, me and all the other gods . . ."

The Ghost under the Necessary House

During the census before last that kicked off the mad greed of the eighties, I received a government questionnaire which wanted to know, among other things, my name, my various numbers, and how many citizens lived at this address. No surprise. I owed this information to Caesar and provided it gladly. But, in addition, the computers of Washington wanted to know how many flush toilets I had in my house. I vaguely understood the social engineering design of the question, but thought it an untoward invasion of a citizen's just privacy. Is it the state's business how and where I do *that?*

I told them "none," meaning "none of their business," smiled sweetly to myself, and returned my census questionnaire. I suppose I have now joined the Appalachian poor, the urban poor, the reservation poor, and various other undifferentiated deprived in a vast statistical study on what programs are needed to bring me up to official code.

Though I am a relative youngster, hardly fifty, I spent the first seven or eight years of my life in the forties walking west of the house to the narrow white erect rectangle with two holes inside that sat beneath the shade of an old cottonwood and a row of Chinese elms. I felt neither deprived, humiliated, nor needful of Washington's help or advice with the business I had at hand. Sometimes I felt cold in winter, in a great hurry to finish the job and go back to the stove, and sometimes threatened in summer by the squadrons of mosquitoes and flies that patrolled the air space outside the half-mooned door.

Most farmsteads in the Midwest until perhaps the sixties still had the old outhouse sitting at a discreet distance from the house, and even though modern plumbing had, by now, arrived, it was still pleasant on breezy summer afternoons to sit outdoors with a novel or, if you were a teenager, a forbidden magazine like *Playboy*, enjoying the solitude and privacy of the wooden bench with the familiar smells coming up from underneath.

A whole school of jack leg domestic outhouse architecture and decoration developed: small luxuries and amenities that added a little elegance to that most fundamental of human experiences. Some had fine screen doors, others had shutters for light and ventilation. I have read books in outhouses by candlelight and by kerosene lamp. My friend, Carol Bly, recently built a new outhouse with a skylight. "The stars!" she sighs, "are magnificent." Some outhouses are brightly painted; some prefer fashionable weathering. An old Norwegian immigrant built a five-holer for his son, wife, and their three children. He measured each behind and sanded the pine until it was smooth as marble. A gift of love and ingenuity! I never inquired whether the family ever simultaneously sat in that emblem of togetherness and solidarity, but since they were Norwegian and reserved, I doubt it. Still, the idea was lovely. A tavern in Wilno, Minnesota, had matching gender-sensitive outhouses with a canine motif: Pointers and Setters. Years ago I went there for a beer with a woman friend from the city. "Where?" she asked. "Out back," said Wally. A minute later, she came into the bar with a puzzled look, "What am I?" "You pick," said Wally, muffling his guffaw.

The outhouse has made its way into the world of literature, too, particularly, I suppose, on the treeless prairies where the plainest facts of

life are inescapable. Here, everything is visible, and you ignore it at your own interior peril. Robert Bly, who went to a country school himself and learned well the finger code for the journey out into the weather, notices a metaphor or two in his "Outhouse Poem."

> *The schoolhouse lies anchored near the road.*
> *On each side, floating, two white outhouses,*
> *like delicate outriggers.*
> *Two thin paths worry away to each.*
> *How marvelous to think of the two sexes,*
> *each with their separate bottoms,*
> *out here on the treeless plains!*
> *There are two sexes! It's a fact!*
> *It's a fact with a white door.*
> *It's a fact with a hole underneath.*

Jim Heynen, who grew up among conservative Dutch farmers in northwest Iowa, reminds us that as with the automobile, telephone, tractor, or computer, not everyone greets the arrival of technology and progress with joy, and that Luddites have an argument, too, even about modern plumbing.

67

WHO DIDN'T WANT AN INDOOR TOILET

When times got good, everybody got indoor toilets. Most people kept the outdoor privy too for when the weather was nice or for when their feet were too muddy to come in the house. You had to be a pretty bad farmer not to be able to afford an indoor toilet.

Except one rich farmer. He didn't want an indoor toilet.

When other farmers asked him why he didn't have one, he told them things like this.

Houses are places where you go to have good times with your family. To eat. To sleep. To play with your children. To make children. Now you people with your indoor toilets, what have you done to your houses? You put a place for people to shit in them and call it improvement! Think of this—somebody says, I have to go to the toilet, and instead of going outside, they just go into the next room. Now how are the rest of you supposed to feel when you know that person is right on the other side of the door—only a few feet away—shitting! At least people with chamber pots could hide them behind the bed. But your indoor toilet is always there. Pretty soon your kitchen smells like shit. And you call that modern! You call that civilized! A house is almost a holy place. Now you tell me what kind of person would build a room for shitting in a place like that! Not even a dog shits in his own house.

Nobody could argue with him really. They just tried not to talk about toilets with him. Because when they did they couldn't help feeling a little bit foolish for what they had done to themselves and their houses.

However foolish, indoor plumbing has triumphed, and most of the remaining outhouses are battered and deserted, not even worth the trouble for neighborhood hooligans to tip over on Halloween. Who would enjoy the havoc? Who would curse and vow revenge?

Only ghosts . . .

Outhouses were as personal, makeshift, and peculiar as their owners. Built, maintained, and moved according to taste and necessity, they contain in their architecture and furnishings one microcosm of the settlement of the prairies. Perhaps these humble ghosts are worth looking at and thinking about after all.

The ghost of the outhouse is imbedded in our childhood language, too. I grew up in a house where Icelandic was the first tongue of adults. I learned to ask for a bathroom in my old relatives' houses by asking for the *kamar*, after which they pointed in the right direction, indoors or out. When my mother, Jona, went in her sixties to Iceland for the first time to have a look at her father's farm and the neighborhood mountains, she particularly enjoyed speaking her elegantly old-fashioned Icelandic, and having natives ask her how long she had been away from home. "Never been there in my life," she answered smugly. One night, I took her to the fanciest spot in Reykjavík, Naust, a high-toned fish restaurant with decorations from old ships. The waiters wore tuxedos and presented with great flourishes wine lists bound in leather. They behaved as if Reykjavík was Vienna or Paris, and the ancestral rock pile a center of European culture and sophistication. Jona made her way nicely in Icelandic, even flirting with the resplendent waiter, until she asked him in complete innocence: "Hvar er kamarin?" It seemed a simple enough question, but the waiter's face reddened and he blurted out an explosion of Icelandic. "Where the hell do you think you are? This is Reykjavík, not the boondocks!" Jona had just asked for the outhouse in the Icelandic equivalent of the Plaza Hotel.

She knew no better. Her Icelandic was a century old. When her father emigrated in the 1880s from the poorest, remotest corner of this already poor and remote rock pile, Icelandic farmers had no words for

flush toilets, nor for radios, cars, telephones, or even electricity. She was born with perfect grammar and a fine accent, but a twelfth-century vocabulary. Her own twentieth century happened in English, as it did for so many children of immigrants.

Kamar seemed a suitable enough word in my boyhood, and is still not without its charms. In this it resembles the outhouse itself, which when the twentieth century and its technology occasionally collapse, remains a serviceable building. We ought not to sniff at the functional simplicity of our own past in our obsessive state-of-the-art snobbery.

The Chinese don't. They regard an outhouse as a treasure, a fertilizer factory that sweetens the grain and vegetables at no expense. Those who have eaten both Chinese tomatoes and American winter baseballs understand the virtues of paying attention to night soil and honoring your outhouse.

Outhouses, like other old buildings on a farmstead, leave ghosts behind them in the soil. Archaeologists of the future, investigating our lost and botched civilization, will regard outhouse ground as one of their richest sources for digs. False teeth, lost jewelry, coins, catalogs and newspapers, tobacco cans, whiskey bottles, forbidden novels, the whole detritus of our culture that will explain us to the future, lie buried behind every house. In Minneota, where the ground remembers the weight of glaciers and freezes deep every winter, spring thaw will bring you unexpected gifts from your outhouse. I have found two Indian hammerheads and a half dozen turn-of-the-century soda bottles with rusted iron stoppers in my garden. Be alert for your own treasures working their way up from underground in the spring sun.

A few years ago, I decided to plant an asparagus patch in my back yard. I asked the advice of an experienced gardener. "The richer the soil in organic nutrients, the more the asparagus loves it," he said. "Why don't you plant it where the old outhouse stood?" The asparagus that rises as if by reincarnation every May seems visibly pleased with all those human ghosts rumbling around underneath. It is fragrant, sweet, and tender, eaten raw. It takes more pleasure in human beings and their history than we sometimes do ourselves.

The Virgin on the Farmall— The Venus in the Chevy

The measuring of an age in centuries and decades has become a kind of bad mental habit, a filing system gone berserk. We cut and trim history and reality to fit our generalizations so as to make neat sequences and invent catchy tags. The "twenties," the "roaring, dirty, thirties," the "wartime forties," the "sleepy fifties," the "revolutionary sixties"—or worse yet, the Age of Reason, the eighteenth century, as if in 1799, the central committee met to formally give up faith in reason and decide (as a committee might put it) to go into machines in a really big way. The metric or decimal division of history is frequently as graceless and inane as metric weights and measures. Imagine the metric version of these familiar phrases:

31.103 grams of prevention are worth .373 kilograms of cure; I love you 35.238 liters and 8.809 liters (a bushel and a peck); walk 1.609 kilometers in your neighbor's shoes before you judge him; .473 liters of beer, if you please, kind bartender.

A foot is not only a unit of measurement; it is attached to your body. A yard is not only three feet; it is where we all go to lie at last. History, too, goes awry when it loses its connection to our own bodies and to daily experience. One of the obligations of having been born with a brain and eyes is to make our own historical demarcations, our own tags, and then to put them modestly before our neighbors in order to see if our experience touches theirs in enough ways to be worth thinking about.

To that end, as the twentieth century, or the second millennium, starts putting on its overshoes for the long trip into the night, I propose that we call this: The Age of Failed Machines, or The Age of Iron Litter. Drive down any farm road in Minnesota or anywhere in the Midwest, or for that matter, anywhere in America. Where trees grow at all, there's a small grove around the farmstead, sometimes only a few stray boxelders and cottonwoods, sometimes something more grand and orderly, usually the gift of the Department of Agriculture. The denser the grove, the harder you will have to look at sixty miles an hour, but trust me, reader, you will find it. In that grove, or behind the weathered corncrib or next to a rock pile, or in brazen places unashamedly visible in the front yard, sits the shrine of dead machines. There, in various conditions of rust, decay, and squalor lies a '49 Ford or a '53 Chevy, or an International truck, or a rotted manure spreader, or a hayrake with oxidized tines, or an F-20 iron tractor, or a drag, or a combine, or a plow. Sometimes there will be a little paint left so that you can tell a green John Deere from a red Farmall. Sometimes the car or pickup will be a wrecked heap, clearly towed to its final resting place. Sometimes it will have chugged in under the last power in its clotted cylinders, a favorite truck that finally gave up the ghost, took the last trip out back, and intends to go no further, at least in this world.

Machines and human beings have this in common: When age, broken parts, and advances in technology bring them to the end of their usefulness, you have to put them somewhere out of the way. They cease, to use eighties' language, to be viable; they can't work any more; it's too expensive to feed them or, even at a pittance a ton, to drag them down the road to the scrap-iron dealer. It costs more to move them those miles than to shove them into the grove and let them compost at their own pokey speed. For a while you might need a part or a bolt off their corpses, so you can visit them, crescent wrench in hand, and do a little recycling. But after a while even the bolt sizes change, and the rust is too thick. So in the lonely majesty of their graveyards, they wait for the second coming when old machinery shall be greased and oiled again in a glorified body.

How strange these metaphors of theology sound when used to describe old machines rusting in a grove. However ridiculous it seems at first, I ask you, dear reader, to think again, and to drive around the section or to the outskirts of town, and have a look. What you see back of the grove may be an American saint's relic, a shrine, a visible history of the rise and maybe the fall of a spiritual idea that operated in all of our lives whether we knew it consciously or not.

Henry Adams, the turn-of-the-century historian and philosopher, certainly thought so. In 1900, he went to the Paris Exposition where he saw a display of dynamos intended to celebrate the industrial achievements of the last half of the nineteenth century and the glittering promise of technology in the newborn twentieth. Adams was then sixty-two, a curmudgeonly Bostonian, a mistruster of progress, probably a closet Luddite. But he was no fool.

To Adams, the dynamo became a symbol of infinity. As he grew accustomed to the great gallery of machines, he began to feel the forty-foot dynamos as a moral force, much as early Christians felt the Cross.

The earth itself seemed less impressive to him than the power of the dynamo.

Before the end one began to pray to it; inherited instinct taught the natural expression of man before silent and infinite force. Among the thousand symbols of ultimate energy, the dynamo was not so human as some, but it was the most expressive.

He called the dynamo an "occult mechanism"; I would call a steam thresher, a Model T, or a John Deere tractor by the same name. Adams, too, mistrusted the conventional labeling and sequencing of history, but he had a stubborn mind.

He insisted on a relation of sequence, and if he could not reach it by one method, he would try as many methods as science knew. Satisfied that the sequence of men led to nothing and that the sequence of society could lead no further, while the mere sequence of time was artificial and the sequence of thought was chaos, he turned at last to the sequence of force; and thus it happened that, after ten years' pursuit, he found himself lying in the Gallery of Machines at the Great Exposition of 1900, his historical neck broken by the sudden irruption of forces totally new.

He compares the machine force of the dynamo with the force of the Virgin and Venus in the Middle Ages, here felt only "as sentiment. No American has ever been truly afraid of either." Venus "was goddess because of her force; she was the animated dynamo; she was reproduction—the greatest and most mysterious of all energies; all she needed was to be fecund." Fecund indeed . . . how many children of Cyrus McCormick, Henry Ford, John Deere, Charles Dodge, and J. I. Case populate the landscape? We are probably more afraid of power takeoff than of the *ewigliche weibliche* (the eternal feminine). A baler can eat your arm, but a statue is a statue.

The Virgin and Venus in Europe have generated the highest energy ever known to man . . . yet this energy was unknown to the American mind. An American Virgin would never dare command; an American Venus would never dare exist.

What might Adams think of the dashboard Virgins in pious cars, or of the Playmate Venus odor-eater hanging from the mirror of the truck cab? Small reminders of the power of one energy transposed to another? Adams and his friend Saint Gaudens the artist go to look at the Virgin of Amiens near Paris. About this Adams speaks sadly.

St. Gaudens' art was starved from birth, and Adams' instinct was blighted from babyhood. Each of them had but half a nature, and when they came together before the Virgin of Amiens, they ought both to have felt in her the force that made them one, but it was not so . . . Neither of them felt goddesses as power—only as reflected emotion.

Instead "they felt a railway as power."

As Americans, we have tried in this century to make our machinery into Virgin and Venus together, the emblems both of our spiritual and sensual lives, and the true force that holds us together as a culture. Yet it seems to me that, like Adams, we have failed—have grown only "half a nature." How many virginities were lost in a car? How much sexual energy is expended in "laying a little rubber," and goosing the foot feed of a souped-up Pontiac with glass packs in the muffler? How many rites of passage do we undergo in getting our first license, our first car? Why do we name our cars and give them characters, as if they were creatures, or talismans? Turn

your radio dial to a country station late at night on a lonesome freeway—you will find the liturgical music of trucks playing for you.

Farming, particularly, has invested not just its trust, but its faith in every religious sense you can imagine into divine machinery. Drive down any township road in farm country during growing season; you will soon find yourself stopped dead behind a tractor or combine the size of a small house covering both lanes. Behind it, like iron octopus tentacles, a plow, drag, or cultivator spreads out over the road shoulder and half the ditch. You will have a long time to drive slowly and admire the force, energy, sheer size and grandeur of that machine. It costs a fortune—likely more than your house and accumulated savings. It is powerful and efficient beyond anything you own. Nature, in some way, is no match for it. It is the gladiator that has conquered manual labor, leaving only the defeat of chance and circumstance. It seems likely to bring even weather under the dominion of its mammoth tires. The farmer who pilots it ("drive" is too timid a word for that iron behemoth), owns a debt that would shock you in its magnitude. You, poor soul, could never borrow that much money! To own that machine requires sacrifice and heroism. It is not a thing but a kind of Grail. Yet, look at the evidence of the countryside with a cold eye. In fifty years, that gargantuan combine will be a rusted ruin, showered by cottonwood fluff in summer and sheathed in ice all winter. When the next behemoth is born that can harvest your beans in forty-five minutes flat, your current behemoth will suddenly become unsalable scrap iron. The heroic steam threshers, plows, tractors, rakes, binders, swathers, grinders, spreaders, balers, cultivators, ad infinitum, of a hundred or even fifty or thirty years ago, sleep silently in the grove, ghosts that have outlived one technical revolution or another, their force spent, their energy

leaked out, their dynamos drained.

Those machines were, in some way, false gods. They relieved what Karl Marx called the mindless brutality of rural life, but as in every bargain you sign with Mephistopheles, he wants a price. In the case of farming, the price is debt, overproduction, wasting and depletion of the topsoil, and the necessity for growing large and specialized. Even forty years ago, farming was still a dilettante's pleasure if you wanted it to be—a little of this, a little of that, and a little idling, too, if you were not consumed by greed. A little corn, a little flax, some oats, some hay, some pasture you've never plowed, a hundred chickens, a few ducks, a few milk cows, some feeder cattle, and a leavening of pigs to add charm and fragrance. Large machines put an end to that sort of life. Once you have sunk money into the machinery, you must use it efficiently, or you will soon be farming on the Henry Thoreau model with a hoe in a borrowed garden. There is some question about who owns whom, or who is whose servant: you or your machine? Who gives orders, and who expects to be obeyed? If we give force and energy not to Venus or the Virgin, but to the dynamo, it will ask us some obeisance in return.

But a part of us venerates those old machines, as if they were saints' relics in old churches. The Midwest in the summertime is full of threshing bees and old machinery shows where lovingly preserved or restored equipment is started up, allowed to deafen and delight an audience with its noise and thunder—the putt-putt-putting of the gods—and then paraded down the main street to be admired. "Now *that* was a tractor," says the old codger in the crisp new bib overalls, as the 1915 J. I. Case three-wheeled 1020 model with the four-cylinder vertical engine booms and clanks by on its iron wheels. He has seen a mystery, in every sense of that word—a mystery that once had true force as Adams understood it, and that mystery has brought the old codger joy. What more can you ask of a relic?

I grew up on a farm in the forties already decorated with dead machines, and still farmed, in the opinion of many neighbors, by machines my father should have allowed to die natural deaths long before. He taught me to drive a tractor on a Farmall whose only concession to modernity was rubber tires to replace the old steel spokes. He had spotted his son early as an incompetent, and the old Farmall was, in his opinion, the only tractor on the place slow, heavy, and untippable enough to be proof against my addle-headedness. He was right; I never managed to tip it. Its turtle speed and mechanical unreliability assured my escape from work that had to be done quickly or well. For this, I was grateful.

My father was also a Luddite—I come by it genetically—and no lover of solitary work that interfered with his social pleasures: card playing, story telling, and a little whiskey. The horses were gone by the time my memory begins at the end of World War II, but I heard a wonderful story from my father's hired man from the early forties. According to Ralph, my father preferred horses to tractors and always loudly maintained that together with his team he could do more work than any damn-fool newfangled tractor. He bought one anyway, and sent Ralph east on the tractor while he took the horses west. They used to place small bets on who could plow the most acres in a day. The horses were by this time well past their prime, though my father refused to send them off to the rendering works. Ralph invariably won the bets, and by 1945, the horses had disappeared into legend and probably glue. I asked Ralph why my father, no lover of labor for its own sake, clung to

his horses for so long. "He liked them because they knew him," Ralph said, "and besides, he always figured you couldn't scratch a tractor's nose or feed it sugar." My father seemed to have miraculously preserved the half of his nature that Henry Adams thought lost in Americans. I didn't appreciate it enough as a boy, so I owe him some praise now.

What is true of our faith in farm machinery in the Midwest is true of cars over the whole country. It's no longer safe in America to make generalizations about gender, but I'll make one anyway. I think even humorless ideologues might have a hard time finding fault with it. Ask an American man to name the cars he has owned, and to characterize them and describe their peculiarities. Then ask him the same question about human beings he has made love with. The first answer will be richer in detail, affection, and accuracy, and the answer to the second query might even lead back to more detail on the first. Touché, Mr. Adams. I offer no comment on this phenomenon except that it describes something about us that might cause some psychic difficulties. Our real Venus rides not in the front seat but under the hood; our virgin sits not on the dashboard but instead keeps the pistons company.

Whatever else failed in this century, the automobile triumphed. No use questioning its victory. There are more of them than of us, and we design our cities not for our convenience, but for theirs. A rise in the price of meat or grain has no serious political consequences, but double the price of car food: Regimes topple and careers collapse. Their graveyards are a little uglier than ours, stuck in a worse neighborhood maybe, but what can we expect? They are bigger and stronger than we are, and their bodies contain less water so they decompose more slowly. As we see the cars of our youth, in my case, the classic '57 Chevy, the '59 Cadillac with the big fins, the failed Edsel, the disappeared De Soto, they remind us of our own aging. They are not so sensitive to us, though, and speed by our graveyards without a second glance from the headlights or even a small trembling of the hood ornament.

But Americans, of course, love a winner. Almost everyone is dead who might have a memory of America without paved roads snaking even into relative wilderness, gas stations (now convenience stores) numberless as stars, and traffic jams in the middle of nowhere. We *are* our cars or our pickups—a Buick is something to believe in, Ford has a better idea, what's good for General Motors is good for us. Our driver's license is our national identity card, our certification of adulthood and citizenship. We pray in our cars, make love in them, bank in them, eat in them, glory in them. What we have not quite figured out is what to do with them when they die.

On farms we keep them, put them in an out-of-the-way spot, and let them be. Sometimes, as age overtakes them, they become beautiful and we photograph them by moonlight, lonesome half-wrecked machines with metal eye sockets and wrinkled fenders. The old red truck is our version of the equestrian statue or the monumental arch. We nod as we pass by to do chores, and remember good times and close scrapes. We measure our lives by their progress at sinking into the topsoil to wait for the next glacier. Phebe Hanson grew up in a Norwegian parsonage in Sacred Heart, Minnesota, in the thirties. In this poem, she remembers waiting in a neighbor's grove while her mother lay dying of TB. These cars seem likely to outwait even the glacier, biding their time until the second coming.

COTTONWOODS

In the cottonwood grove
behind Dahl's farm
the eyes of rusting cars
stare at me before
I crawl into them,
pretend I am driving;
power flows from the wheels,

I believe I am in control,
forget my mother's heart
lies fading in the little bedroom
beyond the rows of corn.

They have sent me away
from her dying to play in the grove,
to sit in old cars,
to whisper into the ears of corn,
towering above me as I sit between the rows
reading her letters
which say she misses me,
even though it is quieter without me
and my brother fighting.
He has brought her a goldfish
from the little pond
beside the pergola house
and laid it on her stomach.

Years later I return to the grove,
where the cottonwood trees
have grown scrawny,
but the old cars are still there,
their eyes stare at me,
unseeing and dead.

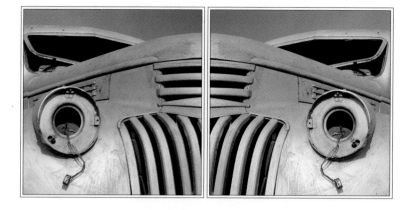
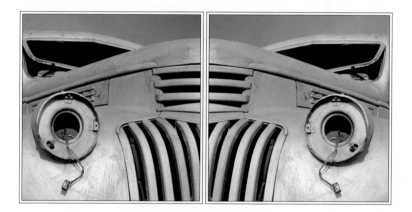
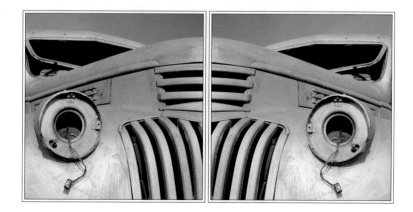

Sometimes we love cars enough to bring them back to life. Gordon Brekken, the father of a friend of mine, collects Studebakers and restores them. For him, a Studebaker is not only a car, but a moral and aesthetic choice—a touchstone by which we judge beauty and good sense. He adorns his everyday cars (alas, no longer Studebakers!) with a bumper sticker: "Keep America Beautiful. Drive a Studebaker." His farm shed is half full, not of practical machinery, but of old Studebakers in various stages of repair. He covers them with plastic to protect them from dust and cold. He studies classified ads for Studebaker parts and keeps his eyes attentive when he drives by junk yards. He subscribes to *Studebaker* magazine, reads it faithfully, and drives long distances to Studebaker rallies to show his cars in competition and "talk Studebaker" with those who have risen to moral consciousness. I once told him about a junked pink Studebaker I discovered behind a bar in Bozeman, Montana. He wanted to know the model, the year, and a rough parts inventory, and grumbled at my foolishness when I couldn't provide them. Americans, as Henry Adams knew, take force seriously even when they don't find it in old cathedrals. Adams says that "all the steam in the world could not, like the Virgin, build Chartres," but it built Studebakers and that, as my friend's father might say, is something not too bad. Even if we don't build the Cathedral of Chartres, we need the courage to love what we do build. Here's the American question: Why can't God be as easily manifest in a Studebaker as in a statue?

My cousin, Daren Gislason, gardens with the same passion and intensity as my friend's father collects and cherishes Studebakers. He appropriated land from neighborhood farmers along the Yellow Medicine river, and made a garden the size of Versailles, miles of trails through boxelders, willows, and unplowed prairie, decorated with beds of iris, tulips, marigolds, wild flowers, native grasses and bushes, God's plenty of flora. He collects the junk of Minneota to recycle in his garden. Every hundred yards there's an old couch or a chair, half decomposed but still serviceable, where strollers can take a rest and contemplate virgins, dynamos, Studebakers, or whatever else is on their minds. About fifteen years ago, unknown neighborhood wags decided to play a practical joke on him. They hauled the corpse of a black '39 Plymouth seven miles north of town and plopped it in the middle of his garden. He remained calm; he's a man who understands the Zen of gardens and accepts the unusual gifts of the universe on their own terms. He planted bluebells on the hood and windshield, started a native cactus garden on the black roof, installed raspberry bushes behind the trunk, and used the interior to store hoes, rakes, spades, pails, and birdseed. Within a few years, the old Plymouth was transformed from nature into art—witty recycling, the only sort that matters. Visitors came to be photographed with their foot mounted on the fine and still intact old running boards, yellow cactus blooming behind their hair.

The cactus perished in a wet year, but by then native prairie had almost overwhelmed the Plymouth. It has turned into a black iron ghost being eaten by grass, a fine metaphor and still a much-loved prop for local photographers. Hailstorms broke out a window or two, but the front seat still provides a happy home for garden tools. This Plymouth is junk transformed by love and a sense of humor into something like a shrine. Only a fool would try to answer the question: To what? I don't know, and neither do you.

In Alliance, Nebraska, dead cars have been consciously transformed into a shrine. Carhenge is a replica of Stonehenge, the old Druid shrine in England, but here built not from rock but

from everything from a '58 Cadillac to a '79 Honda—all painted stony gray to resemble their ancient namesake. As in Lourdes or Canterbury, you can buy postcards, tee shirts, and bric-a-brac at Carhenge. Imagine Henry Adams, now three-quarters of a century dead, reincarnated to visit Alliance, Nebraska. What might he feel? Adams "complained that the power embodied in a railway train" (he might have updated that to a Cadillac . . .) "could never be embodied in art." Adams had, of course, seen the real Stonehenge, one of the oldest sights of force, energy, emotion in Europe. Would he have laughed at this kitschy imitation of spiritual power? Would he have thought Carhenge a poor try at restoring the lost half of his nature? He would have been both right and wrong: right in that Carhenge, of course, is pure kitsch, a joke at the expense of the Druids. It requires no genius to understand that.

And yet . . . and yet . . . the builders of Carhenge made better than they knew. If indeed we live in a century that has worshipped machines, technology, a better mousetrap for a better universe, then we live also in a century that has seen incontrovertible evidence of the failure of all those machines: the car, the steam engine, the hydrogen bomb, the personal computer, and the cuisinart. Our gods don't work. Probably the last generations of them didn't either. But just as we honor J. S. Bach, Søren Kierkegaard, Thomas Aquinas, the unnamed architect of Chartres, Silbermann the organ builder, and the anonymous crafters of windows, so do we owe the Cadillac and the John Deere a little honor, too. All of them gave us energy—humor, intelligence, beauty, force (to use Adams' word), and if the energy has leaked out of them a little now, it's time for us as humans to imagine a new force. Meanwhile, something worth a look is decaying in the grove behind the barn if our eyes are open to see it.

The Last Insult of the Glacier

I asked a shirttail cousin of mine what he thought of rock piles. We were at a Gislason family reunion in the front yard of an old farmstead in western Minnesota, wild hot August wind blowing Styrofoam cups, brownie crumbs, and fried chicken bones halfway into the next county, and ringing in the hearing aids of the elderly Icelanders.

"What?" he said quizzically, his lack of apprehension not entirely the fault of the wild, noisy wind.

"Rock piles?"

"Yes, rock piles."

"Why in God's name do you want to know *that?*"

"I've been thinking about them. We're only a quarter of a mile from the old Snidal rock pile. I have an odd friend who likes to take pictures of it."

He scrunched his nose a bit and then half bellowed over the wind gusts, "Think of the energy it took the glacier to eat all those rocks and then move them so far. It must have gotten tired and set them down here."

My cousin is a city man, so he is able to look at rock piles from the glacier's viewpoint, even expressing a little pity and fellow feeling for the two-mile-thick gritty ice that once lived here, gasped, died of heatstroke, then leaked away into the Gulf of Mexico through the Minnesota River Valley.

I feel no such aesthetic distance from rock piles. Like anyone who grew up on a western Minnesota farm, I hate them. They are a heavy symbol of brainless labor, a reason to despise spring—even in

a place with seven-month winters. When the frost goes, rocks rise. They lie scattered all over the north eighty like a mine field, ready to sink your drill or your cultivator. So you pick them up, put them on a hayrack, drive to the fence line where your ancestors planted the ur—rock pile for you so that the sins of the fathers could be visited unto the children for numberless generations. Bend and pick, drop and bend, pick and drop, bend and pick, ad infinitum, ad nauseam, and then comes winter, and then spring . . . bend and pick . . . "Enough!" I said early. There'll be no numberless generations of this nonsense. Rock picking and hog-house shoveling made a poet—even an intellectual—out of me. Every hour of your life you spent with rocks—work that would have bored the be-Jesus out of a moron—was a wasted hour. I wanted books and a one-way ticket out—to somewhere where the rocks could damn well stay where they pleased until they had paved the topsoil and seeded a mountain. In dark moments, I even hoped for another glacier—fast. O come Lord, and visit this mile of ice unto the heads of mine enemies . . .

After twenty years' escape from the sight or thought of rock piles, I found myself back in Minneota, teaching in a college not far away that hadn't existed when I left. Like some huge mental boulder left buried deep by the glacier, the college surfaced while I was off having adventures in the East and on other continents. What thaw caused that? I thought to myself. Yet, here it was not fifteen miles from my father's rock pile, a building full of poets and writers. One of them, Phil Dacey, is a Saint Louis man. He moved to

Cottonwood and must have gotten drafted for rock picking by one of his farmer neighbors. Having grown up without my savage hatred for rock piles, born of hard experience, he was able to look at them wryly, dispassionately, with even a certain detached pleasure. I admire this poem, but I could not have written it.

PICKING ROCK

Renters pick fast and loose;
if you own the land, you pick close.

You can pick a field clean one year,
come back the next, and find more.

They rise up from somewhere far below.
Just how far, I don't know.

It's a rain,
but slow, and upside down.

The higher up you get,
like this tractor seat,
the easier they are to spot.

Sometimes I think there are
pregnant ones down there.

Most are granite, some are limestone.
This is no work for one person alone.

There's one kind, blue-black,
that's twice as heavy as it looks.

This one looks like a brain.
Somebody was thinking too hard again.

Here's an old Indian hammerhead.
You can see where the leather strap fitted.

Sometimes it seems everywhere you look
there's a rock.

At the words "find more," I would have broken into ritual cursing. We all remain prisoners of our childhood in at least some ways, until the day we die.

I took more visceral pleasure in a story I heard from Marc Wignes in the M & M Cafe in Ghent, Minnesota. Twenty-five years ago, state road crews began the job of rebuilding the roadbed for highway 68 that connects Minneota and Ghent with the rest of the universe. The roadbed had been eaten away by too many heavy grain trucks, too much freezing and thawing, too many internal combustion engines. We live in a weightier century than we imagine. Partway into the job, the crew ran short of crushed rock. The roughly crushed stones with their jagged edges were necessary for a solid roadbed. Hot tar mix likes to stick to the rough surfaces, hardening into a firm glop. It slides off smooth-sided stones, thus causing the potholes and cracks that sometime lend a little excitement to motoring in Minnesota. So the crew dispatched a tough old German, built like a fireplug, who could chew snoose, cuss, and talk deals in the right language. He cruised the countryside in his pickup, scouting for sizable rock piles. He drove into farm yards and dickered.

How I'd have loved to see the expression in any farmer's face when he was offered hard cash for a rock pile. Minnesotans are masters at hiding delight, looking phlegmatic and detached at what others might take to be moments of intense passion and joy, but I don't think they could have hidden their grins at the thought of selling rock, for cash, and having someone else move it with large equipment.

Another old German from Canby felt differently about his rock pile. He refused to sell it to the fireplug. "I put too damn much work into that rock pile to let you just haul it away for a

song." The pickup moved north to the next farm. If a man is attached to the visible ghost of his own labor, there's no bargaining with him. Local farmers evidently still cherish the memory of the old German rock dealer. Farms became rockless up and down the highway, and some fence lines saw sunlight for the first time since the turn of the century.

It's pleasant to think of all that mindless labor being finally and unexpectedly rewarded, a harvest of rocks joining a harvest of corn and beans. Some, overcome by greed and possibility, might even have imagined rock futures, or markets for feeder rocks. The WNAX radio market reports might go like this: barrows and gilts, cutters and canners, crushers and stackers . . . A grandiose schemer, with some historical underpinning, might have dreamed up pyramid sales for rocks.

It's a pleasure also to think of all that rock I hated so much being useful at last to human beings. When I heard the story of the highway 68 roadbed, I began driving on it with more happiness, imagining the weight of my tires pressing down on the crushed head of a field stone some bored farmer's son like me picked up and piled onto a hayrack on a spring day forty years ago.

Yet, my photographer friend who fell in love with the Snidal rock pile is right, too. Both beauty and history live in rock piles if we keep our eyes open. A rock pile is democratic; it houses not only rocks, but tin cans, ruined furniture, machine parts, broken sinks and bathtubs, old shoes, chipped dishes, Maytag tubs, five-gallon pails with holes in the bottom, scrap lumber, single work gloves, beer bottles, and livestock bones. That's our own history, piled up with the glacial detritus.

There's a moral in rock piles, too. However much we disapprove of history, and wish it to be different, it exists; it is heavy; it is boring work to clear the fields over and over, but if we don't do it, nothing will grow, and it will break our most glorious technology with its hard facts. We simply have to pick it up, and put it somewhere to remind us. Glaciers come and go, and so do we. Meanwhile, there's corn to be planted and who knows? A road crew might start work; an old German in a pickup with a coffee can in the front seat might drive into the yard and make us an offer.

96

Petrified Chin Music

Tourists seldom include western Minnesota in their travel plans if they are interested either in good weather or looking at antiquities. The weather is terrible. Always. Everything is new. Almost. What about the Jeffers petroglyphs, pipes the local antiquarian or travel agent? There are, indeed, ancient petroglyphs just off the county road east of Jeffers.

Though I grew up not sixty miles away and thought myself an inveterate traveler and surveyor of antiquities, I was forty-five before I ever made it to the petroglyphs. My friend David Lee, the Utah poet, is a petroglyph hound, and when he first visited western Minnesota, insisted on seeing them.

"But it's late November," I protested weakly, "and there's a nasty wind from the northwest."

"Coward . . ." he said.

We left for Jeffers, armed with cameras.

We followed the signs, but still managed to drive by the petroglyphs on the first pass. There's not much vertical drama to stop the eye on the Jeffers road. We walked the few hundred yards across the bare prairie, cameras clutched in wool mittens, turning our faces away from the wind's bite. Despite the arctic gale, no snow had fallen yet, so we were in luck. We could still find the petroglyphs under our boots.

A man once took his ten-year-old son to see the Grand Canyon for the first time. The boy glanced down quickly over the south rim and said to his father: "I thought it would be bigger . . ."

What would the poor boy have said if we had taken him to the Jeffers petroglyphs? Even the sink hole of contempt has a bottom.

The petroglyphs, like so many of the signs and leavings in this landscape, whether human or natural, require the cooperation of your imagination if they are to reveal their wonders. They also require your active curiosity—a quality almost atrophied by television, and discouraged by institutions like state, church, school, and probably your family.

Look down to find the petroglyphs. They are supine, rough stick figures gouged into hard red Sioux quartzite. Some look a little like animals or hunting figures, but they as easily could look like other things—wine jars or dancers. They might be a pictographic language, or they might not. The only thing archaeologists say with certainty about them is that they are old. They must be newer than eleven thousand years, because until then, two miles of glacier sat on top of them and it would have had sufficient strength in its icy arm to erase them. European settlers arrived just over a hundred years ago, but certainly no bored immigrant farmer chiseled them for fun. Since they are postglacial and prehomestead, that leaves a possibility gap of 10,850 years or so when *someone* carved them. Who? Not the Dakota. Not the Ojibwa. No one knows. Some humans who came through and stayed for a while some time in the ten-odd millenniums. They didn't leave much information, just some rough ghostly signs whose meaning is now forever lost. Kilroy was here, but he was close-mouthed. The petroglyph hunting party

took a few unsuccessful photographs, mumbled and speculated a little, thought of the rich petroglyph cliffs of Utah, turned up their coat collars against the wind, and retreated to the warm car and a nearby steak house for whiskey and large meat. Outside the door of the steak house hung signs with a Viking ship, the head of a bull, and the name of the house of the Norse Gods–Valhalla. That's the way sign hunting goes in America.

Before the next glacier arrives to clean the slate, I wonder what mysterious signs and remnants of our language we will leave for the new evolutionary round of archaeologists? I'd guess that our commercials will outlast us, though their frailer material will be gone long before Sioux quartzite. In some future laboratory, white-coated assistants might piece together faded bricks, weathered boards, and metal shards like a jigsaw puzzle with the box cover lost.

"Look," says the young archaeologist in the year 2452, her eyes full of the delight of discovery,

This one says **BULL DURHAM.**
This one says **COCA-COLA.**
This one says **MADISON'S BEST FEED.**
This one says **PENNZOIL.**
This one says **CHAMPION SPARK PLUGS.**
This one says **JESUS SAVES.**
This one says **2,568 MILES TO WALL DRUG.**
This one says **L.S./M.F.T.**
This one seems to be a kind of poem, though we can't decode the language:

> **PRICKLY PEARS**
> **ARE PICKED**
> **FOR PICKLES**
> **NO PEACH PICKS**
> **A FACE THAT PRICKLES**
> **BURMA SHAVE.**

Drive into almost any small town in America. If it has a brick commercial building: a bank, a hotel, a dry goods store, then one exposed wall of that building is almost certainly painted with an advertisement. Many of the products and services advertised are now long dead, only ghost brands; some survive and even prosper in new forms: Bull Durham, Coke, Pepsi, Key Overalls, Pillsbury Flour, Lucky Strikes, Spearmint Gum, Grainbelt Beer. As the paint fades, a curious thing happens for which I have no scientific explanation. For example, a Coke sign, minus seventy-five percent of its paint, intensifies as it ages. It almost seems to grow in size. The red can or fluted bottle seems bigger, grander, brighter, cleaner, as if the message had sunk into the brick and started to glow from inside. This happens to some humans, too, as they age. At eighty or ninety, their faces look on fire with intensity. It's a fine thing to see, either in an antique painted sign or in an old human being, and is one of the reasons both are photographed so often and lovingly. Even the Jeffers petroglyphs were probably duller a thousand years ago, when "it was all new in through here."

Walker Evans took what are arguably the most famous American photographs for his book with James Agee, *Let Us Now Praise Famous Men.* If you have a copy at hand, leaf through it. There are only about sixty pictures, but they plunge from eye to heart as few photographs have ever done. What do you remember? Faces, old boards, shoes, horses, shabby furniture, ramshackle buildings. Look once more at the walls of those buildings: Nehi, Coke, 7-Up, Groves Chill Tonic, and more. Evans' focusing eye loved those imitation petroglyphs painted on the sides of broken-down stores in rural Alabama. About a third of the greatest American photographs announce the availability of soda pop. The power and sharpness of those images has not diminished since 1936.

Now, look at Bob Firth's photograph of a Spearmint pack with a gremlin glowering over it. Though the paint is almost gone, the white Spearmint pack seems enormous and vibrant. The gremlin was probably once a cuddly Wrigley kid, but he's aged into a gargoyle. Next to his gremlin's head in letters almost dimmed to gibberish—or a lost incantation—the sign says: "SEALED IN ITS PURITY PACKAGE–THE FLAVOR LASTS . . ." You could find the gremlin's brother leering off the cornice of a Gothic cathedral. The imp of the perverse beckons you to have a pure chew—freshen your breath a little. It's like Dracula's invitation to have a glass of wine. He never drinks—wine. Think twice about chewing. Yet the sign, in its tumescence, is a visual delight. What message will it leave to the petroglyph hunters of the future?

My friend, the poet John Rezmerski of Eagle Lake, is a connoisseur and collector of roadside ad signs. He savors them for their humor, their invention, their language—both visual and verbal. They are the word made flesh: poetry with a body. They fit comfortably into John's theory of American poetry, the "Chin Music" of our culture. John explains.

CHIN MUSIC

When I was a little kid, every once in a while on our way home from fishing, my Dad would stop at the bar down at the Volunteer Fire Department—East End Hose Company—"down at the hose hall," we called it. I'd get to perch on a barstool and swill orange pop while he had a beer before we went home. There was always a bunch of men hanging around, usually watching baseball on the TV at the end of the bar. It seemed natural for them to be watching baseball—they had names like Shorty and Beans and Froggy and Bud. I was Lefty's kid.

There was always an argument or two going on. Usually one about sports, and one about politics. I never understood exactly what they were arguing about. Once, when we left, I asked my Dad to explain. He said, "Aw, they don't even know what they're arguing about—that's just chin music. They just like to listen to their teeth rattle."

After that I always asked him, because I liked it when he said "chin music." He'd always vary it a little bit: "They're just making chin music. They like to hear their cheeks flap." Or: "They like the sound of their gums slapping together." I got very fond of my father's chin music. And anybody else's.

Years later, when I started publishing poems— at first, the kind of bookish poems that are hard for anybody except an English teacher to pretend to understand—my Dad would read them and shake his head. He never said it, but I could hear him very clearly: "So you're going to spend your life fooling around with this chin music?"

Chin music is like any other music—it can be played badly or well. But you like it most when you play it yourself. I learned it pretty well. Here I am getting ready to tell you about my childhood and my crazy dreams, for no good reason except that I like to hear words gurgling over my teeth like orange pop, and to hear meanings going every which way like an argument at the end of the bar. I just like to hear my jawbone practicing the scales.

When words rub against each other they make noise, and that noise is chin music . . . Chin music is all around us—on the infield, at work, in books, in bed . . .

A sign decaying on the wall of a building or nailed to a fence post or plastered to a billboard becomes a species of petrified chin music, or if you prefer, American mercantile petroglyphs. Though they have disappeared from the roadside, Burma Shave signs may be the most-famous and well-remembered American poetry. First ask your neighbors over forty to recite four lines of Robert Frost—or Emily Dickinson or Walt Whitman. Then ask for a Burma Shave jingle. Who wins? Ask for the visual symbol of the God Zeus; then ask for the Bull Durham logo. Again, who wins? There is no right answer to the second; Zeus and bags of roll-your-own share the bull.

With the death of Burma Shave, our most-famous and omnipresent signs announce Wall Drug, on the edge of the Badlands in South Dakota. I suppose that there is a Wall Drug sign on the Greenland Ice Cap and at the source of the Nile, announcing how many miles you have left to travel to get free ice water. John once drove from southcentral Minnesota through most of South Dakota with his notebook open. This is the poetry he found.

POEM FOUND CROSSING MINNESOTA AND SOUTH DAKOTA

Read Village Voice at Wall Drug.
Ice in jugs. Free. Wall Drug.
Cheeseburger at Wall Drug.
Western bookstore at Wall Drug.
Wall Drug. You can't beat it.
Western wear. Wall Drug.
No squawk if you stop at Wall Drug.
The friendly spot. Wall Drug.
Homemade donuts. Wall Drug.
Hot Bar-B-Q. Wall Drug.
Rockhounds stop at Wall Drug.
Get your boots at Wall Drug.
See gunslinger at Wall Drug.
Wall Drug. Kids love it.
Cowboy quarter. Lifesize animated. Free at Wall Drug.
Silver dollar display. Wall Drug.
Cokes. Wall Drug.
Ice at Wall Drug.
Wall Drug. Strongly recommended.
Film—all types. Wall Drug.
We try harder. Wall Drug.
Wall Drug. A hot deal.
Wall is well at Wall Drug.
Wall Drug back yard.
Rootbeer under the trees. Wall Drug.
Free ice water at Wall Drug.
Stamps wholesale—Wall Drug.
Coffee. Wall Drug.
Wall Drug loves company.
Wall Drug Store believes in America—buy U.S. Savings Bonds.
You can't lose with a winner. Wall Drug.
Would you believe? Wall Drug.
Start Badlands trip at Wall Drug.

Free Badlands history. Wall Drug.
Viewmaster reels. Wall Drug.
Charburgers. Wall Drug.
Bring your smile and appetite to Wall Drug.
Wall Drug open 5 a.m. to 10 p.m.
Since 1931. Wall Drug Store.
Two eggs and toast 35 cents. Wall Drug.
Eat under the tree at Wall Drug.
Art Gallery Cafe—Wall Drug.
Wanted: You. Wall Drug.
Wall Drug in 10 min.
Malts at Wall Drug.
You have missed Badlands——stop at Wall Drug, information.
Only in America. Wall Drug.
Wall Drug in 3 min.
Let's stall, here comes Wall.
Dinosaur exit for Wall Drug.
Free Free Free Indian exhibit. Wall Drug.
Tired? Stop at Wall Drug.
Wall Drug exit one mile.
Don't miss the Wall Drug exit.
Here comes the Wall Drug exit.
Slow down. Wall Drug exit.
Wall Drug and Badlands, this exit.
Wall Drug four blocks.
If you would like one of our signs
to display at your home or
place of business, just ask the clerk.

Until the glacier comes back, I have a feeling that these signs will tell us more about ourselves and our culture than any government statistical abstract. While they mellow, fade, and chip away into inscrutable petroglyphs, we still have the pleasure of reading and looking at them, and that, unlike anything they ever advertised, even the ice water, is free.

Cutting Slices out of the Wind

What makes a book of pictures interesting is what cannot be photographed. This is equally true of poems, essays, and stories; their energy is in what cannot be said. At some point, if our lives are to have any weight, we must learn to both trust and imagine the invisible. We must honor silence by listening closely to it.

Here is an example. Take a picture of a windmill, or look at one that someone else has taken. You know what it is: a tower with a wheel on top to catch the wind. The wheel has a kind of sail attached to it and slanted vanes. You have read *Don Quixote* and chuckled at the mad knight jousting with the windmill. Perhaps you've been to Holland, famous for windmills.

You know what it does: the wind turns the wheel and pumps water up from the earth. Before electricity was common, windmills powered generators. On still nights, you read by candles. Sleepy cows stood next to the windmill, drinking from the water tank. Boys in winter were sent out to the windmill with hammers to crack the ice for the cows to go on drinking.

Look at the picture again. The windmill looks inert, frozen, still. If the photographer has set a long shutter-opening on a windy day, perhaps the windmill is an elegant blur, suggesting motion. You know that windmills move and the picture stands still. But you are, after all, not crazy like Vincent Van Gogh who tried to paint light and motion—on windmills, among other things. He cut off his ear and shot himself. You prefer calm pictures that make

suggestions, that have implications, that do not try to grab nature by the throat and, by God, move it.

Yet, nature is, if nothing else, a moving. If you live in the flat middle of this continent, exposed on both northern and southern flanks to great whirling storms, mad chaotic contradictory masses of air going where they please, then the central fact of your life is wind. And you can neither take a picture of its moving nor write in any human language its noises. The old song directs you to "Call the wind Mariah." Call it anything you please. It won't come. Not at your bidding anyway.

I once saw an aerial photograph of a section of land after a tornado moved across it diagonally. It looked like the Palmer method of penmanship for malevolent giants. The tornado had scrubbed a swath of landscape clean of everything on it—buildings, machines, grass, grain, humans, trees—leaving only violent but orderly swirls in the dirt. The wind is not always friendly, but then neither are works of art.

Look again at the picture of the windmill. Imagine metal rattling and clanging. Imagine the whirring of the wheel blades, the gushing of water, the creaking of the tower. Now you have done a little interior work, and have something closer to a windmill in front of you. The picture taker or the word maker can only begin your labor. Human beings fool themselves into thinking that they do their work alone. Everything human is done in tandem with other humans—and with the wind, among other things. When we

112

sign our names to something we make—Firth, Holm, Van Gogh, Cervantes—we sign it in wind.

As oil energy peters out, speculators in the middle of the continent have rediscovered wind—the great and inexhaustible power. New windmills rise everywhere, handsome steel shafts topped by something that looks like a sideways helicopter. They stand in long rows, whirling in unison, giving birth to electricity. Power begats power, and if everything works right, a little profit, too. Why not run a farm with wind? Soon there might be wind markets, wind futures, wind that takes credit cards, charges interest, pays dividends.

Retired windmills still decorate the landscape. Sometimes their rusting vanes pump up only noise, a sound and fury signifying nothing but itself. Sometimes the wheel has blown off, leaving the tower with an amputated head. Those windmills were good servants to the wind, and sometimes to men; if men forgot them after their usefulness, the wind remembers and rubs and tickles them everyday, chatting about old times, water rising, and cattle they have known.

But a picture of a windmill at rest is only half a windmill—less, maybe. Gail Rixen, a poet who lives in a windy Minnesota place, Chokio, and knows what can't be said, tries to say it anyway.

PICTURES OF THREE SEASONS

The camera eye is never my eye—
too distant, too late.

I wanted to show you
pheasants and blue jays fighting in the dead garden.
I had a sequence of sunsets, looking southwest,
five days of brilliance defying dull drifts.
And there were pictures of me,
hair done up, laughing—
you wouldn't know me.

All this I tried to save in your absence
through long days working in dim attics
and in the heat of a drought summer.
Somehow the pictures do not show what I saw.
Something about the lack of light
or slow film or the distance.

You see here shapes hung in gray air,
light and shadow
and faces caught on bad sides,
just two dimensions requiring explanations.

You really should have been there.
I swear there was more.

There's always more, but that's your work. You can't depend on the wind for everything.

Towers Rising from the Floor of the Sky

We're a little short of height on the tall-grass prairies. The people, mostly north European, tend to be oversized, and the corn reaches eight feet in a good year, well over your head. But our towns and farmsteads are low and horizontal, probably designed in unconscious harmony with the calm oceanic swells of the prairies, so long-breathed in their rising and falling that we imagine ourselves living on a vast perfectly flat green pool table. Too much soaring might insult the landscape, so we practice a sort of architectural reserve and keep things low to the horizon.

What would Chartres, Canterbury, Notre Dame, or York Minster do all day around here—bare their fan vaulting to the sky or tickle cloud bottoms with their spires? We're glad the Sears Tower in Chicago, the Eiffel in Paris, and the IDS and the Foshay in Minneapolis all stay where they belong. We visit them, sometimes with pleasure, but we like more modest buildings as neighbors.

Writer Howard Mohr imagines a Philadelphia burglar, "the best second-story man on the Atlantic coast," sent to western Minnesota to breathe the good air for his health. His health probably improves, but he's a little melancholy at the thought of home. He says, "Most of the towns don't even have second stories." The widow of the old Norwegian banker in Milan, Minnesota, refused to move out of her grand three-story Victorian mansion, so she simply amputated the top two floors, finishing out life where sensible people stay: close to the ground. Architects and preservationists wince at the sight of the truncated house, but I suspect her neighbors said to themselves: "Well, she was an old lady and all those stairs were hard for her. Besides, who wants to walk all that way up just to sleep or go to the bathroom? And, think what she saved in fuel oil . . ."

Practical to a fault, we make two exceptions to our mistrust of height: the grain elevator and the silo. I don't know what it says of our inner life that most of our churches and houses are earthbound, but when grain and silage for feeder cattle enter in, we allow a little soaring. Probably it says nothing.

There are differences between them. A grain elevator is an upright rectangle with attachments; a proper silo is a round tower with a dome. A grain elevator is a public business, in the old days often a cooperative, and in Canada still labeled "Grain" or "Wheat Pool." A silo is a private enterprise that you build for yourself, according to your own taste and ambition. A grain elevator stands most often in the center of a town, always next to a railroad track (or now in the age of vanishing railroads, a ghost track); a silo lives on a farmstead, always next to a barn, as a pantry is next to a kitchen. A grain elevator is a public landmark, the only way in a flat and treeless prairie to see from one town to the next and get your bearings on distance and direction; it is not just a storage bin, but a navigational aid. A silo is a more private matter; it announces by its size and majesty the relative prosperity of the farmer, the magnitude of his herd, but it does not get you from

one place to another.

They share visual grandeur though, rising above their neighbors without apology. For beauty, I prefer silos, but then I prefer the circle to the square. It seems to me a truer description of the way things actually work in history and the universe. At any rate, elevators and silos present you with a Gnostic choice: the Great Mandala or the Pythagorean right angle.

A grain elevator wants decoration, even makeup, on its great flat face. Unadorned, it can never quite shed its utilitarian expression. It *is* its work, and there's an end on it, as Sam "Dictionary" Johnson might say, if he had ever seen one. The new fashion in Minnesota is to hire a muralist, buy him an odd-thousand gallons of paint, and turn him loose. Good Thunder, a town of only a few hundred, close to the Minnesota River, did so, and the result is grand, indeed. They hired the Black mural painter Ta-Coumba Aitken, originally from South Carolina, and instructed him to paint an enormous portrait of the town's namesake, the Dakota chief, Good Thunder, and then to surround the old boy with smaller scenes from local history. The result is a sort of eighth wonder of rural Minnesota. Mr. Aitken managed to paint a solemn utilitarian elevator wall with gaiety, humor, and light. If I farmed close to Good Thunder, I would be proud to install my wheat behind the chief's nose. I like the idea, too, that a Scandinavian and German town hired a southern Black artist to decorate the temple of Anglo-Saxon capitalism with Dakota scenes painted in colors of Gypsy vibrancy. Whoever imagined it wasn't a curious and funny experience to be an American? The multicultural Mrs. Grundys have got it wrong—it is not a matter of solemnity, but of pure gaiety and divine laughter, to turn the mixer on high and stir the melting pot into a mad froth. Good

Thunder saved and honored its only skyscraper in splendid style. Now the elevator can soar like York Minster as it damn well pleases.

Silos are by nature more shapely, more elegant, made from more beautiful materials—the oldest ones of stone, and afterwards clay, varicolored brick, massive concrete blocks, and sometimes wood. You do not need to decorate a face lucky enough to be born with beautiful skin. Nature will do; art can bide its time. Some farmers gild the lily though. One of my favorites is a brick silo east of Saint Peter that was painted thirty years ago as a Coca Cola can. As a college student, I drove by it on the way to Minneapolis and liked its red brassiness, but always thought the silo handsome enough without its gilding. A few years ago it turned into a 7-Up can with a dome, the sacred soda now garbed in green.

A silo is a curious contraption, the most exacting of farm buildings, as dangerous, sometimes even deadly, as it is lovely. Silage is simply fermented livestock food—most often corn or alfalfa, first chopped, then packed in tightly and sealed. While a silo is being filled, and for a few weeks afterwards, the fermenting silage gives off nitrogen dioxide, a yellowish brown gas that smells like laundry bleach. It is perfectly capable of killing either you or your cow. James Whitaker's agriculture textbook warns us that "as a safety precaution, it is wise to keep the silo shut off from the barn for ten to fourteen days after filling, and to make certain that the barn is well ventilated. No one should enter a tower silo without first operating the blower for fifteen to twenty minutes to purge any accumulation of silage gas. Two or more persons should be present for safety." The last sentence sounds like a warning to swimmers about shark-infested waters.

And yet, that deadly gas is given off by the richest and most efficient food for fattening the beef you eat. The silo is after all only a convenience that allows a farmer to safely store a vast supply of food for a vast herd of cattle. The more silage, the more rib roasts. The expense of the stored silage explains the great care with which silos are built and maintained. They are the tightest of farm buildings, all doors, openings, and walls meticulously sealed, the silo sides bound with tight hoops of steel. A fine silo has never been cheap; it demands your attention regularly if you wish not to kill yourself or your cattle, or worse yet, ruin your investment.

A 1993 state-of-the-art silo will probably be made either from glass-coated steel or fiberglass reinforced plastic. I love best the brick silos from the twenties and thirties. In a sea of wood buildings—only the Catholic Church and the banker's house were ever made of brick—the fine, sometimes even ornamental brickwork, the rich red color and shining dome glowing in the winter twilight made me think I had wandered out of the flat Protestant Midwest and into the ghost of a medieval city. If the farmstead itself fell into ruin, the house turned into a practice target, the barn leaned over so far it collapsed in on itself, the silo invariably outlasted the destruction, and stood sturdily, looking as if it were only drawing a breath to stand up for the next thousand years.

It was the guard tower of an ancient castle that had survived wars and invasions and had stories to tell. I imagined narrow spiral stairways inside leading to the dome, slit openings for archers to pepper the invading army with arrows, and in a room at the top, a sad and beautiful young girl—the king's daughter—combing her long black hair while she waits for a brave

knight. Maybe in the crypt under that silo slept a dragon . . . Anything was possible in a silo if you let your mind's eye loose to move.

In fact, only gassy hay or fermented corn mash would ever have kept the king's daughter company, and the invading army would have been Holsteins, Angus, or Herefords knee-deep in manure, violating the twilight silence with long mooing, cud noises, and wet belches.

The countryside where I live is peppered with fifty- or sixty-year-old silos boldly signed with the big bronze letters A.C.O. For years, I wondered what that mysterious acronym meant. I asked a farmer one day in a cafe if he knew the history of his neighbor's silo. "A. C. Oaks," he said, "an old silo company out of Sleepy Eye. Those were rich men's silos. Even a tornado couldn't budge them."

The silo, like the internal combustion engine, saved labor, and became one of the instruments of the farmer's baptism into the world of growth, size, and debt. If A. C. Oaks had left his heraldry on your farm, you could buy whole armies of feeder cattle, then hope for the best from the market. One of my favorite A.C.O. silos stands in aristocratic solitude surrounded by scrap lumber and plowing. It has indeed survived a few tornadoes, hailstorms, blizzards, and lightning strikes, but it had trouble

with the collapse of cattle prices. Maybe the most violent storms take place not in the ionosphere, but on the business pages.

I always wanted to live in a round silo. In the dominion of the square low house, I felt that by turning, turning, you might come 'round right. Minus the nitrogen dioxide and old sour hay, a silo looked a fine place for thinking, maybe even writing poems, with a few wraparound windows, and a stained glass dome.

Round towers seem always to seduce writers and philosophers. When W. B. Yeats was fifty-two, he bought Thoor Ballylee, a Norman tower on the Irish coast, from Lady Gregory. After he had made enough money touring America to restore it for himself, he wrote his poem, "Blood and the Moon."

I declare this tower is my symbol; I declare
This winding, gyring, spiring treadmill of a stair is my ancestral stair;
that Goldsmith and the Dean, Berkeley and Burke have travelled there.

The American Robinson Jeffers liked stone towers, too, his own writer's silo. In his poem about Tor House, he declares:

If you should look for this place after a handful of lifetimes . . .
Look for foundations of sea-worn granite, my fingers had the art
To make stone love stone . . .
My ghost you needn't look for; it is probably
Here, but a dark one, deep in the granite, not dancing on wind
With the mad wings and the day moon.

C. G. Jung, the psychologist, seemed to have thought Bollingen, his round tower in Switzerland, was his mother, or at least his unconscious.

Gradually I was able to put my fantasies and the contents of my unconscious on a solid footing. Words and paper, however, did not seem really enough; something more was needed. I had to achieve a kind of representation of my innermost thoughts and of the knowledge I had acquired. Or, to put it another way, I had to make confession of faith in stone. That was the beginning of the Tower, the house which I built for myself at Bollingen . . . The feeling of repose and renewal that I had in this Tower was intense from the start. It represented for me the maternal hearth . . . There I live in my second personality and see life in the round, as something forever coming into being and passing on.

Something about life in a windowed silo seems to have given writers the power to "declare," to have saved them from mumbling. Fred Manfred, Minnesota's novelist of Siouxland, of epic stories of the settlement of the Midwest, wrote his long-breathed loud-voiced novels in a hexagonal tower. Fred grew up looking at silos. I've never heard of a novel written in a square grain elevator.

Even a round building has two sides. Missiles, after all, live in silos, too. Drive across North Dakota, just south of the Canadian border; the empty grassland is fortified for some hypothetical apocalypse, massive concrete casings loaded with fire and death. Now that America is short on enemies, and brinkmanship has become unfashionable, maybe we can fill those shell casings with sour hay and restock the landscape with a few million buffalo.

I think a woman's view of silos—or of the towers of Yeats and Jeffers—is different from a man's. Nancy Paddock of Litchfield, Minnesota, imagines a farm wife suffering from prosperity. Her husband, like D. H. Lawrence's little boy in "The Rocking Horse Winner" hears his farm constantly whispering: "There is never enough . . ."

124

THE SILOS

All week she watched
the silo grow from concrete slaves.
He had to have it,
this seventh silo—
(each one larger than the last).
And now they line one side of the drive,
half-circling the old house
with a great question
she dares not ask.

That house
with its drafty kitchen and slant floors—
nothing but a shelter for the night
when no work can be done.
(Real time spent with machines.)
He said, when they were married,
eighteen years ago this spring,
he'd tear its boards to shedwood and kindling,
build her a real home
on the wooded knoll.

But now that hill is planted
straight in corn
rows up one side and down
and as the sky fades,
fragile as a broken
robin's egg,
silos loom around her
like black corridors
a woman could get lost in.

That poem states the realists' view of silos. But the romantic view is true, too. David Bengtson, a Minnesota poet from Long Prairie, knew even as a child the proper use of empty silos.

THE MAN FROM COAL LAKE

On warm summer nights he walks to the silo to sing.
While the barn slowly sinks into itself, the silo is tall and strong and still
the perfect place to sing.

He brings white candles and some matches and climbs into the silo, empty
now since most of the cows were sold.
He lights a candle, pushes it into the packed silage, and begins to sing
quietly.

The sounds of old hymns ascend to the roof of the silo.
Sounds that soar forty feet into the air and return to surround him like the
pines deep inside the woods.
There is no sound like the sound of a silo singing.

His voice carries outside to the hills, into the woods, across the lake, where
it joins with the sound of the bared roots of old oaks, the sound of corn
squeaking in the garden, the sound of two sorrel mares standing close, the
sound of pine needles dropping, the sound of jumping fish.

On a night like this he brings a good supply of candles.

Why not singing in a silo? Or an old barn? Or even a grain elevator? Maybe the contrast of tall buildings in low places is there to remind us that at least two things are always simultaneously true in this world. Things only go haywire when we try to turn them into single vision and Newton's sleep. Why shouldn't Bach chorales and nitrogen dioxide live together in a silo? Even prairie types need a little elevation, a place to climb up forty or fifty feet so that you can look down at the ghost of your own practical everyday head. Maybe you should have a little music to accompany the ascent.

The Visible Dead

America could hardly have done better for a common language than English. All the myths we believe about ourselves as a country and a culture, while they may be only a quarter- or half-true, otherwise are completely accurate as descriptions of our language habits. English was born of a miscegenated marriage of elegant French and blunt Saxon; it has no morals or standards; it takes any bastard word from anywhere into its house and lets it breed; it opens its arms to the poor, the tired, and the homeless with far more joy and ease than the country itself ever mustered. We are a kind of Ellis Island of language; words came through our doors and, with greater speed and efficiency than most inhabitants, melted down quickly into common speech. As a result, our word horde is vast and many-leveled—maybe the vastest of any language in history. Since we are spiritual Texans to a fault and love to boast of size and magnitude, American English presents us with an opportunity to tell the truth for a change.

But one gift from our outsized polyglot language is the power to shade and dissipate meaning almost into vapor. Geniuses at euphemism, we find softer, vaguer, more disconnected words for facts that seem unpleasant to us. We pass away, go to rest, or are interred in Sunset Memorial Gardens or some such place, where the lawn is meticulous and stones don't show bad manners by visibly standing up to be counted. Perhaps not by coincidence, two of our distinguished literary reminders of the hard facts of death, both linguistic and otherwise, Jessica Mitford and Evelyn Waugh, were British, the custodians of our language before Americans opened their doors wide to the world's linguistic riffraff. If we want to take a little of the sting out of death and make the grave think twice about victory, we will damn well do it! It's a free country! Why else would we have thrown all that tea into Boston Harbor?

The euphemisms of death, however, are city luxuries of a habited place with money, distractions, and other matters on its mind. On the plains, in immigrant places, the visible graves stand up not in memorial gardens, but in graveyards. They exist in plain Saxon, not having cultivated French manners to soften and civilize them. A yard of graves. That's what they are . . . a field of bones, stones, and language that contains some information maybe useful to us, if we are alert to it.

In the Minneota countryside, you can do a rudimentary ethnic census, a social and economic history, a survey of aesthetic taste and religious preference, all on a Sunday afternoon saunter down township roads. Investigate the graveyards and question the stones. You will find the inhabitants cooperative—up to a point.

There are three kinds of rural graveyards. The first kind huddle around their country church like a field of petrified corn. Sometimes, since rural churches have gone mostly the way of rural schools and given up the ghost themselves, the church will have disappeared from its foundations, leaving only the graveyard. Do these churches evaporate as the parish ages and the town church beckons? Some burn on windy nights, leaving only naked foundations; some have their lumber recycled by thrifty farmers into barns and houses; some are sold, then picked up and moved to new spots to become churches for

younger more enthusiastic denominations; some simply collapse into handsome ruins, and are left for the graveyard maintenance committee to clean up.

The Icelandic Lutheran church in Westerheim township, where most of my relatives are buried and where I am a small landowner myself, closed its doors in the early fifties after the neighborhood Icelandic farmers had moved to town, sent their children off to college and away from the farm, or failed to breed a new generation of steady firmly rooted Lutherans. The Church Board, finding the old church sound of limb, sold it to the Baptists, who had more fervor and more use for a previously owned church. I can't remember whether I was there at the moving or not, but the story is so locally notorious that I made myself a retroactive spectator. The movers successfully moved the church off its foundations and onto a flatbed for its trip down the county road. All was ready, the power lines disconnected in the right places, and the sheriff's lights flashing to head the slow procession. The flatbed inched forward with caution and majesty; after a few feet, the sturdy-looking Icelandic church collapsed in on itself with dramatic finality with great clouds of dust. Poor luck for the Baptists . . . "Just like a damned Icelander!" muttered one old farmer. "Too proud and bull-headed to move . . ." But the neatly tended graveyard remained on its corner. The stones faced west to supervise the ghost of the dead church that once kept them company.

Sometimes a country church seems never to have wanted its graveyard close at hand, and banished it to the next section on some bare and windy spot. Driving down the road, you are startled to see a wrought-iron fence and a nicely mowed graveyard with a couple of trees to shade the dead, surrounded by a thrashing ocean of alfalfa or wheat. Maybe, the old settlers thought, the dead needed a little privacy, too— and wanted a special trip to visit them. Or maybe the land was cheap.

Finally, there are graveyards themselves, "a fine and private place," sometimes only a grave or two in an open field or next to what was once a farmstead. Why here, alone, rather than in a community of the dead? Perhaps the farmers wanted to plant something more permanent of themselves next to their own crops on their own land. This was, after all, for a great majority of Minnesota immigrants, their first chance in history to be landowners rather than hired hands, even semifeudal serfs who brought up the rear guard of the European class system. If we bury grandpa and the baby lost in childbirth in our own yard, it will give us a tentacle into history; enough graves and the north eighty will become an ancestral estate. Or perhaps there were immigrants so wounded and disillusioned by institutions like state and church that they wanted no truck with them in death, the last great unbureaucratic privacy.

Will Weaver, the northern Minnesota writer, has a wonderful short story called "A Gravestone Made of Wheat," where he posits both of these possibilities. A proud old Norwegian, told by the sheriff that it is now illegal for environmental reasons to bury his wife Inge in his own farmyard, thinks back on a half century of pettiness and abuse from local power, then plows the old lady into the middle of a wheat field by moonlight. She's safe from the sheriff, and her sons will always be able to find her where the wheat is a few inches taller than its unfertilized neighbors.

No township in Minnesota is without these private lonesome graves. They are local touchstones, scenic attractions, and breeding grounds for folklore. Ask at the coffee shop downtown; you'll find out where they are and hear stories. Between Sleepy Eye and New Ulm, a folklorist friend of mine found a grave of a six-year-old girl dead in the 1880s, lying in the middle of a field between two trees, the place reputedly haunted. He had heard local yarns of visitations,

spectres, odd lights, moaning that was not the wind, damp white dresses, and grass that refused to grow. A bunch of us decided to investigate: the folklorist, a couple of writers, a photographer with infrared filters, and a skeptic. We went at sundown and stayed until dark. We drank wine and told stories. The photographer got fine and eerily colored pictures, probably because the earth itself is a fine and eerie place, but the skeptic seemed to have won the night. Nothing supernatural happened except a bunch of friends having a good time at a lovely and lonesome spot. Who's to say that's not enough?

Around my hometown, I send visitors to two grave sites. A single white marble military gravestone with an Irish name and the number of a Civil War regiment stands in a field along the highway a mile from the almost entirely Belgian village of Ghent. Did the Irishman not want to lie down with Belgians? Was he the only Protestant in a Catholic town? The only veteran among pacifists? There are probably answers to these questions, but I am not interested nor, I feel sure, is McQuestion, the dead veteran in his private national cemetery. He is visually handsome in white marble surrounded sometimes by clover, alfalfa, thistles, prairie grass, and sometimes by ice and snowdrifts that almost cover him up. He says "Kilroy was here . . ." by whatever name.

One of my great-granduncles, a homesteader north of Minneota, was a local grandee. He had somehow made money in Iceland, traveled to Denmark, and become worldly before arriving north of Minneota. He indentured his brothers' passages to America (as I have heard the story) and did little work himself. He read, and sent the only two of his many children of two marriages who survived past thirty to the university. The brother and sister came home after his death, tended his farms, read more books, threw nothing away for fifty years, and never went to church. Among their books were Voltaire, Thomas Paine, and Robert Ingersoll, signs of free thinking, and Madame Blavatsky and Anne Besant, signs of theosophical inclinations. Neither of the children ever married, and when they died, in the 1960s, they went back of the grove to join father, mother, and a handful of stepbrothers and stepsisters, all dead either in infancy or early youth. The house, with most of the accumulated packrattery, burned the night after the sale, and the new landowners tore down the now collapsing round barn that once made the farm a landmark. Nothing left but the family graveyard with its almost haughty aristocratic privacy and its nice sense of completeness and finality—all the relatives safely home at last.

It's a wonderful place, behind its fence, next to a muddy river, a little island of the dead surrounded now by a sea of corn and beans, so arrogantly growing, so happily alive. It comforts me a little to see this visible language of graves, to live as its neighbor. A culture that hides its verbal facts will not care very intelligently for its physical facts either. We must both look at things clearly and name them right.

If you want to know something of the history of settlement in a Minnesota township, ask the dead. The living are busy with work, church, or television, and have begun making up new answers, or to put it in an American way: to reinvent the past, to make it "all new in through here . . ."

But the language knocked into marble or granite will give you a few facts if you know how to read them. The road from Minneota through Lincoln County to the South Dakota border goes past graveyards of Icelanders, Norwegians, Germans, Danes, Poles, a scattering of Yankees and Irish, and a few failed Civil War veteran farmers. A few miles in the opposite direction will take you past Belgians, Dutch, and Swedes. If you

ask these graveyards questions, here's a few of the things they might tell you. Who was broke in Europe and when? When did the land in the old country give out? How far had the railroad gotten built? Where hadn't the homestead land run out? Look at the stone piles and the soil quality in neighboring fields. Who got there first to claim the best and who arrived last to inherit the gullies? How many graves of women dead in childbirth or children in infancy? That's a fair gauge of poverty, trouble, and the misery of transplanting. How quickly did English get learned and assimilation start?

In the age of the bilingual education debate ad nauseam, a graveyard will give you a lesson in how assimilation happens. Here's a hypothetical example from an Icelandic graveyard: the history of how the spelling of a common name decomposes.

GUÐMUNDSSON—The original and correct spelling with an odd letter not in the modern English alphabet: *D* with a slash pronounced *th*, and with correct grammar: the genitive double *s*. This name is a patronymic in the old country and is good only through one generation, and then only for sons. "Dottir" for daughters: Gudmundsdottir.

GUDMUNDSON—Now we have taken citizenship for which you need a permanent last name even for daughters who, after all, are not sons, by neither linguistic nor sexual logic. Here in the New World you can't go changing your name every generation to confuse the neighbors and the tax board—unless you are a gambler. Here we must be like our neighbors, even if nothing in our own language demands it. No double *s*, and a hard *d*.

GUDMANSON—Here the name has started to respect American phonetics, no consonantal blocks to slow you down on the road to prosperity and the middle class.

GOODMANSON—Now, it's begun to look like a real American word! Even the ghost of the aspirated *GUÐ*, (pronounced Gvuth), has died away to become "GOOD" in all senses. Ironically, straight hair used to be called "good hair" in the Black community for years. At least the pink Icelanders didn't have to buy straightening chemicals . . . just changed the spelling.

GOODMAN—Almost a politically correct name; half of the cumbersome gender distinction atrophied away like a leprous limb and fallen into the ash heap of our fast history. It now bears only a ghostly resemblance to its Icelandic ancestry and could safely be carved in any graveyard in New England without disturbing the old settlers. That name can go to Minneapolis and get a good job, carry credit cards, own personal computers, and jog!

It hasn't happened yet, or at least I haven't seen it, but that name will soon be GOOD. Something is gained in that process, but something is lost, too. We've got an American now, but without much memory.

This decomposition took hardly two generations, sixty or seventy years. In a city, it might have gone even faster. A few miles down the road from the Icelanders, the Poles had been at work adding vowels to names like CZK for a couple of generations. Soon the Slavs and the Vikings will look so much alike in granite that they won't remember the insults, invasions, and old quarrels over the last thousand or so years. As Europe in 1992 began erupting into its old ethnic savagery, Americans ought to be at least a little grateful for that process.

Memory is the language of graveyards. It is not so easy to carve words in hard stone to as spit them out of a laser printer or fax them on a memorandum. So language becomes dense and heavy—just a name, some dates, a snatch of a hymn, or an old saying. Euphemisms cost too much to chisel so we dispense with them. The old graveyards that populate the countryside in Minnesota—and everywhere—are good neighbors both spiritually and visibly. They are frequently lovely places, filled with fine shadows and angles and light, gifts for the painter or photographer. They contain the rudiments of our common history, reminding us of who we now are, who got us to that point, and what at least one part of our future looks like, if we are able to see it with a steely eye. Finally, on a fine July day, the air perfumed with the damp smell of mown grass, and loud with mourning doves and meadowlarks singing requiem (or whatever those noises mean), it's pleasant to think, as Walt Whitman did, of all this sweet earth being continually fed by all those sour dead. Just another miracle in a long string.

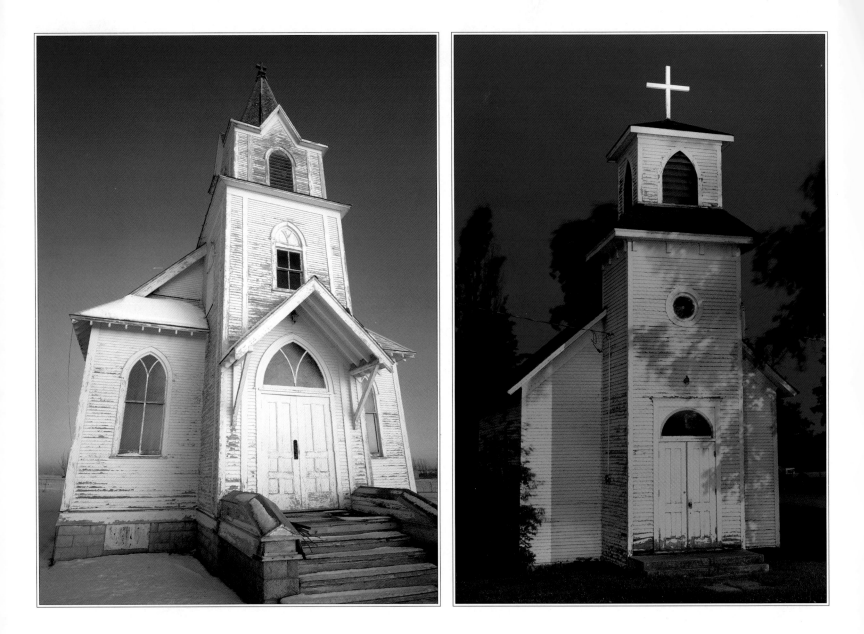

About the Author:

Bill Holm lives in Minneota, Minnesota, where he was born in 1943. He teaches half the year at Southwest State University in Marshall, Minnesota, and travels, writes, and practices the piano and clavichord for the other half. He thinks the only way to see a place clearly is to move a few thousand miles away now and then. From this angle, your home stops looking normal and reveals part of its true strangeness.

Bill has taught American Literature abroad at the University of Iceland in Revkjavi'ic, and at Xi'an Jiaotong University in Central China. He is the author of four—books, two of prose: *The Music of Failure* (1985, Plains Press) and *Coming Home Crazy: An Alphabet of China Essays* (Milkweed Editions, 1990), and two of poems: *Boxelder Bug Variations* (Milkweed Editions, 1985) and *The Dead Get By With Everything* (Milkweed Editions, 1991).

Photo by John Weidman

About the Photographer:

Bob Firth's photographic career began when he was seventeen and his infatuation of "old things" and remnants dominated his imagery. Today, as a leading Minnesota stock and assignment photographer, Bob is best known for his large-format color images of nature, landscapes, and scenics. However, Bob's intrigue with our vanishing heritage continues to attract his camera and lens, revealing his graphic and moody style.

Bob's work is most often seen on calendars, postcards, books, and magazines. His photographs have graced the covers of more than two hundred periodicals. He currently owns and runs Bob Firth Photography and Firth Photobank, a stock photo agency.

Bob, his wife Nancy, and their children split their time between travels, their St. Croix River cabin, and their Minnetonka home.

Photographer's Note:

In these days of "progress" and the apparent need for interrupted farm fields and clean, "new looking" towns, I thank those who allow these ancestral leftovers to moulder in honor, dignity, and most important—peace and quiet. These fine insightful people show respect for the past, present, and future simultaneously, and provide irreplaceable visions for those who see "The Beauty in the Going."

If the photographs in this book bring to mind old places you know and love that asked to be photographed, Bob Firth would like to hear from you! Drop a card or letter or even a snapshot describing the spot to Bob Firth, P.O. Box 1745, Minnetonka, MN 55345-1745. Your old Buick or Grandpa's grainery need to be honored too!